PSYCHOANALYTIC INQUIRY

A Topical Journal for Mental Health Professionals

Volume 10 1990 Number 1

CONTENTS

Converting Psychotherapy to Psychoanalysis

Routledge
Taylor & Francis Group
New York London

Routledge is an imprint of the
Taylor & Francis Group, an informa business

Prologue

CONVERTING PSYCHOTHERAPY TO PSYCHOANALYSIS is relatively commonplace in today's psychoanalytic practice. There are still, however, a number of unresolved questions related to such a procedure. For instance, does the very fact of converting make the subsequent psychoanalysis more difficult or even impossible? If such a procedure takes place, should the patient be transferred to another therapist for the analysis? What are the essentials of psychotherapy and of psychoanalysis that have to be taken into account in such a conversion? For training purposes should conversion from psychotherapy, especially with the same therapist, be allowed for the required supervisory cases?

Many of these questions can be traced to Freud's papers on technique (1911-1915), particularly the following statement: "Lengthy preliminary discussions, . . . previous treatment by another method and also previous acquaintance between the doctor and the patient . . . result in the patient's meeting the doctor with a transference attitude which is already established and which the doctor must first slowly uncover instead of having the opportunity to observe the growth and development of the transference from the outset. In this way the patient gains a temporary start upon us which we do not willingly grant him in the treatment" (1913, p. 125).

This passage can be read not as an absolute admonition, but as

Dr. Malin is Training and Supervising Analyst, Southern California Psychoanalytic Institute and Los Angeles Psychoanalytic Society and Institute. He is also Associate Clinical Professor, Dept. of Psychiatry, U.C.L.A.

a suggestion that the previous treatment would be an interference. We must remember, however, that what might have been called psychotherapy when this was written probably consisted of hypnotic suggestion and other very direct approaches to influencing the patient. With the advent of psychoanalytic psychotherapy, is Freud's suggestion still valid?

Freud's technique papers contain the well-known statements about abstinence and neutrality (1915, pp. 164–165), which are part of the definition of psychoanalysis. Freud warns against "educative ambition" as well as "therapeutic ambition" (p. 119). These papers also contain his statements about the use of the couch and the analyst sitting out of sight, (p. 133) as well as frequent visits, which for Freud meant six days a week (p. 127). To be found there also is the principle of the "fundamental rule" of free association, (p. 107) and the idea of "evenly suspended attention" for the analyst as the necessary counterpart to the fundamental rule of free association for the patient (p. 111).

These various rules and regulations from the technique papers have come to constitute an aspect of the definition of psychoanalysis. Thirty years ago, during my own training, the Los Angeles Psychoanalytic Institute considered it regular practice to transfer a patient in psychotherapy to another therapist for analysis. In recent years that practice has been reconsidered and continuing in analysis a patient one has had in psychotherapy has found justification.

Stephen Bernstein, one of our contributors, brought this concern to the fore with his 1983 paper, "Treatment Preparatory to Psychoanalysis." Bernstein has said that he wrote this paper to justify considering this particular case as one of the required cases in supervision for certification by the American Psychoanalytic Association, demonstrating that only a short time ago an applicant was still not sure if conversion of a psychotherapy case to psychoanalysis with the same therapist would find acceptance by the committee on certification of the American Psychoanalytic Association.

Which brings up another aspect of the procedure of converting to psychoanalysis, one having to do with training and the requirement of supervision of analytic cases. Specifically for this issue of the *Psychoanalytic Inquiry,* George W. Pigman, III, surveyed the institutes of the American Psychoanalytic Association on their procedures regarding acceptance of such conversion for the cases of psychoanalysis required for training. The results certainly demonstrate the changes that have taken place in this regard in the recent past.

The general consensus among analysts seems to be that conversion consists of increasing the frequency of visits to a minimum of four a week and having the patient use the couch. But, as will be seen, even that general opinion is not universally accepted. Gill (1988) and Stolorow (as you will shortly see) question whether these so-called "extrinsic factors" (Gill, 1988) are necessary preconditions for calling a procedure psychoanalysis.

Greenson (1967) differentiated psychotherapies that use the transference to achieve therapeutic goals from those, of which analysis proper is the purest form, in which the transference constitutes the central object of study. This transference aspect of the difference between psychotherapy and psychoanalysis is frequently stated in the various definitions: Psychoanalysis has to do with a systematic analysis of the transference, whereas psychotherapy may use transference interpretations that are selective and partial.

A very significant issue is that of suggestion. Psychotherapy has always been associated to some degree with the use of suggestion. The role of suggestion may range from its conscious employment in supportive psychotherapy to its minimal use in exploratory psychotherapy. But there are problems with using the concept of suggestion as the principle distinction between psychotherapy and psychoanalysis. Gill (1988) reminds us that there is always suggestion in all psychotherapies, including psychoanalysis. He believes that in psychoanalysis we must keep suggestion to a minimum, and we must explore the effect of inadvertent as well as more obvious suggestions that have been introduced into the therapy. For Gill it is the analysis of transference, which includes exploring the effects of suggestion in the treatment, that is essential in the definition of psychoanalysis.

The articles in this issue of *Psychoanalytic Inquiry* deal with some of the clinical and theoretical aspects of the procedure of shifting a patient from psychotherapy to psychoanalysis.

Joseph Lichtenberg and L. David Levi suggest a method of studying the process of changing from psychotherapy to psychoanalysis. They pose a number of questions regarding the rationale for the previous psychotherapy, the characteristics of the technique in the psychotherapy, why the change to analysis, and how the therapy affected the opening phase of the analysis. They propose examining, after the end of the analysis, the effect of the total experience—the earlier psychotherapy, the conversion, and the transference during the analysis—to reveal the impact of previous psychotherapy on a positive or negative outcome. They offer clinical examples to illustrate their approach.

Stephen Bernstein looks at motivation for analysis and working with the resistance to the analysis as a very significant factor in patients who are suitable for analysis but who are not motivated to start with analysis.

Leonard Horwitz describes a case in which the patient was not considered suitable for psychoanalysis during the evaluative phase. After a significant length of time in psychotherapy changes occured that led to a successful psychoanalysis with the same therapist.

Nathan Schlessinger offers a comprehensive review of previous contributions to the subject of conversion. He suggests that the conversion of psychotherapy to psychoanalysis might well be called a special case of "what must take place in any induction into an analytic process." He discusses the diagnostic assessment and offers two case examples, one of which was conversion from psychotherapy to psychoanalysis with the same therapist, and the other in which Schlessinger was the analyst, but the patient had had previous psychotherapy with another therapist.

David Joseph discusses the fundamental rule of free association and its special application to the subject of conversion to analysis.

Alan Skolnikoff approaches the problem from a different perspective, the emotional position of the analyst when the treatment shifts from psychotherapy to psychoanalysis.

Robert Stolorow questions a number of basic assumptions regarding the essential nature of the psychoanalytic process. From his own perspective of seeing the analytic process as taking place in the intersubjective field, he examines (1) the myth of the neutral analyst, (2) the myth of interpretation without suggestion, (3) the myth of uncontaminated transference, and finally (4) the myth of the analyzable or unanalyzable patient.

The final contribution is the aforementioned survey of the Institutes of the American Psychoanalytic Association by George Pigman III.

In an effort to supplement Pigman's findings, I sent in a very informal manner an inquiry to a number of foreign psychoanalytic institutes to learn about their approach to the conversion of psychotherapy to psychoanalysis in the training requirements. The Italian Psychoanalytic Society, The British Institute of Psychoanalysis, and The German Psychoanalytic Institute all say that they do not allow candidates to take cases that have been in previous psychotherapy with them. These three institutes require two analytic cases under supervision in the training, and neither case can have been a conversion from psychotherapy.

The Canadian Institute, on the other hand, does allow candidates to convert their cases into supervisory psychoanalytic cases. They place no actual limit on how long the patient could have been in psychotherapy, but it is usually less than three years. Three cases are required, with no limit on the number of cases converted from psychotherapy, but some people within the branches of the Institute think that only one converted case should be accepted out of three required cases. It seems that 20 years ago there was no conversion, and no particular policy about it either. The Canadian Institute told me, "The difficulty in finding control cases has produced these new policies on conversion of psychotherapy cases to psychoanalysis and this has been set up in the last ten years without any problem being reported by the training analysts."

A communication from the Mexican Psychoanalytic Association says that the Institute holds no official position in respect to converting a psychotherapy case into psychoanalysis; it is left to the discretion of the individual supervising analyst.

The Argentina Psychoanalytic Association has no policy against a supervisory case having been converted by the same therapist from psychotherapy to psychoanalysis. They emphasize that they expect that in such a case the therapist was careful in his psychotherapy technique; hence the major change becomes an increase in sessions per week and the use of the couch.

This is certainly not a scientific sample, but it is interesting to note that the three European analytic institutes do not allow conversion of psychotherapy to psychoanalysis as part of the training cases. However, in Canada, Mexico, and Argentina this conversion is allowed.

REFERENCES

Bernstein, S. B. (1983). Treatment preparatory to psychoanalysis. *J. Amer. Psychoanal. Assn.*, 31:363–390.

Freud, S. (1911–1915). Papers on technique. *S.E.*, 12.

Gill, M. M. (1988). Converting psychotherapy to psychoanalysis. *Contemp. Psychoanal.*, 24:262–274.

Greenson, R. R. (1967). *The Technique and Practice of Psychoanalysis.* New York: Int. Univ. Press.

Arthur Malin, M.D.
Issue Editor

Psychotherapy to Psychoanalysis: A Method of Study

JOSEPH D. LICHTENBERG, M.D.
and L. DAVID LEVI, M.D.

THE SUBJECT OF CONVERTING PSYCHOTHERAPY to psychoanalysis has long been beset by controversy. Often the argument has had a moralistic tone, such as preserving the *pure* gold of analysis and not *contaminating* the transference. Even "converting" has a religious flavor which "shifting" would not. The patient shifts from one form of treatment to another as a patient with back trouble shifts from bed rest to medication, exercise, or surgery. None of these connotations are important in themselves. Their only significance lies in whatever influence they have had in interfering with a consistent and careful study of this common clinical event. Current need demands such a study. If patients who have begun psychotherapy were to be eliminated as prospective analysands, everyone would suffer. Patients would be deprived of a possibly optimal treatment, and analysts and candidates would be deprived of both patients and a challenging experience, all because of unproven assumptions or unsubstantiated value judgments. In this paper we do not aim to prove the worth of shifting, or even its efficacy under certain

---

Dr. Lichtenberg, a member of the Faculty of the Washington Psychoanalytic Institute, is the Editor-in-Chief of this journal.

Dr. Levi is a teaching analyst at the Washington Psychoanalytic Institute, and an Associate Clinical Professor of Psychiatry at George Washington University Medical School.

circumstances; we simply wish to propose an approach to seeking the information on which to base rational judgments.

We believe an empirical assessment of shifting from psychotherapy to psychoanalysis requires an attempt to answer a series of practical questions, the first of which is: What was the rationale for beginning the treatment as psychotherapy rather than psychoanalysis.

Rationale for Starting with Psychotherapy

What was the rational for beginning the treatment as psychotherapy? Why was psychoanalysis not undertaken from the start? Was psychotherapy the "treatment of choice" in the opinion of both partners? To assess the basis for making this decision, a good deal of information must be made available. We must know from the patient's point of view what led him or her to consult a therapist or analyst. This requires answers to two questions: What was the patient's problem? Did he knowingly consult a therapist rather than an analyst, or an analyst because he knew the analyst was one, or an analyst, knowing only that he or she had a good reputation? Still from the patient's point of view, did he come with a conviction about the mode of treatment he was seeking—asking for therapy and not for analysis, or asking for analysis knowing more or less what is required of him, or not knowing?

From the analyst's point of view, did he believe that the patient's problem was best treated by analysis? Was he unsure and thus felt a trial period of psychotherapy would be diagnostically prudent? If he was sure the problem would be best treated by analysis, was the life situation one that seemed to rule it out on pragmatic grounds or the type of character resistance too rigid to consider it at first?

As the *consultation* came toward its ending, how did the perspective of patient and analyst intersect? Did the analyst recommend analysis and the patient refuse? Did the analyst, anticipating a refusal, reluctantly recommend psychotherapy while planning to induce the patient later to accept analysis? Did the patient see his problems as too "minor" to accept analysis as a recommendation, or did he give lip service to his "need" for analysis, but cite pragmatic reasons so insistently that the analyst acceded?

Psychotherapy Technique and Process

What was the technique used during the psychotherapy? How did the resulting process evolve? Was the analyst's approach essentially the same basic exploration he would have employed in analysis? Alternatively, was he more advising, directly supportive, and/or self-revealing than he would have been during an analysis? If advice was given about a practical decision, what was it? Would the context foster subsequent excessive dependent expectation? How were direct and indirect references to the analyst, the work, the experience, and the choice of treatment (that is, transference) dealt with? What indicators were observed that an introspective exploratory process had begun?

Decision to Change

What was the basis for the shift to psychoanalysis? Looked at from the viewpoint of the analyst, what criteria did he use to determine the need for the change, the timing of the change, and the patient's willingness to make the change? From the patient's point of view, was his willingness to make the change the result of increased stability in his life situation, increased awareness of the need for more intensive exploration, and/or an increased trust in the skill and knowledge of the therapist-analyst? Once agreed upon in principle, how were the arrangements worked out; how was the basic rule dealt with? Were any caveats about the difference in expectancies offered? Was it necessary to renegotiate any arrangements such as fee, payment schedule, or payment for missed appointments? How was the use of the couch handled by both partners?

Effect of Psychotherapy on Opening Phase

What was the impact of the previous psychotherapy on the opening phase? Did the analyst feel that his technique changed? If so, in what way? Did the analysand refer to any differences in his experience? How were these references (or their absence) dealt with? Did the analyst pick up any special marker of the transition such as a dream, a bit of acting out, or an anxious question relating directly or indirectly to the change? Most of all, did the previous relationship appear to move seamlessly through the transition? Or did the unfamiliarity of lying on the couch and the greater frequency of sessions have a demonstrable effect? Did the patient, for example, sense the analyst as "different"? Did the analyst experience a change in the patient, for example, that he was less friendly, more open, suddenly argumentative, or more involved?

Effect of Total Experience

What was the impact on the analysis as a whole and its outcome? This may be the most difficult feature to assess. On the one hand, the analyst may have a definite impression that the period of psychotherapy proved to be a necessary, highly useful preparation, which contributed greatly to a positive outcome. Alternatively, the analyst may conclude that a type of interaction, an expectancy, was established in the psychotherapy and consolidated a type of aversive response to deeper exploration so that the analysis was compromised from the beginning.

Another approach to difference in outcome is statistical. Within the analyst's own experience, does he feel that this case fits into the group of patients shifted from psychotherapy with whom the outcome has been favorable? How would he compare the outcome of his own cases begun as analyses to the cases shifted from psychotherapy where he has been the therapist and/or where someone else was the therapist? Using pooled data and a broader research methodology with follow-up interviews, can any features—length of treatment, outcome within diagnostic groups—be discerned about cases where psychotherapy has preceded analysis?

Case Example:

Sally M, a 30-year-old accountant, came for treatment because she did not want to make the same mistakes with her current boyfriend, Bill, that she had made with her former husband. Recently she had believed herself to be pregnant by Bill. After discovering she was not, she had become depressed and lost interest in her work and in her ambition to become a partner in her high-powered accounting firm. She thought she might really prefer a home and family.

She is attractive, soft spoken, at times tearful, usually serious, but sometimes playful. She showed ability to distinguish her immediate emotionally determined sense of reality, for example, of the analyst's being critical, from more fully validated perceptions.

She finds stable support and strength in her father while she feels more ambivalent toward her mother, who is more emotional but who, with her self-derogating and self-sacrificing style, induces guilt. Sally's father was away in the army for six months directly after her birth. Her mother was ill and away for five months when Sally was only 18 months old. Thereafter, for some time she would not let her mother out of her sight and recalls a childhood fear on trips that her parents might abandon her.

While her father was in graduate school, her mother had to work, and Sally at three and a half was sent to nursery school. She recalls being the last one to be picked up to go home. Before age six, she was coming home alone to fix her own lunch.

She recalls sudden alienation from a devoted boyfriend in high school as an early instance of what she has since repeated and is concerned about. She always worked hard and did well in school, college, and postgraduate work, thus gaining entry into her prestigious firm and recognition for probably advancement.

After an intensely emotional but repeatedly disappointing three-year relationship with a college mate who could not commit himself, she acceded to marry a handsome but immature young man, Tom. She was devoted at first, but his diverging social interests hurt and disappointed her. After two years of marriage she became intensely involved with an older married man with whom she often worked closely. He was strong and decisive, whereas she saw her husband as weak. However, he was also cold. She feared that divulging his identity could cause him damage. After six months of weekly psychotherapy with a woman social worker, she felt comfortable enough to separate from Tom. Her man friend, however, though his marriage was on the rocks, was not ready for commitment. She had met Bill six months before consulting with the analyst. He is warm and sensitive. Though the relationship with Bill is comfortable and might lead to marriage, she feared being again drawn to the cold man friend or someone like him.

During the four sessions designated for evaluation before a decision on longer-term treatment, Sally showed some capacity for introspection and psychological mindedness and seemed to find some relief in being able to articulate thoughts and feelings to an understanding listener. She seemed primarily motivated, however, for quick help in deciding about Bill and dealing with the relationship with her man friend. She also wanted help deciding what to do with her change of feelings about her work. From her history and pressure in the sessions, the analyst picked up her disposition toward action rather than interest in deeper internal satisfaction. He wondered about her distrust, as in her withholding her man friend's identity. The analyst did not then know the full early history and wondered if her problems could be adult developmental vicissitudes, which might be resolved with less intensive therapy. In going over treatment options, he mentioned analysis, that is, treatment requiring four to five sessions per week as a possibility. However, he had the thought that, given her suspiciousness and her disposition to action rather than toleration of dysphoric feelings, she might have left analysis had it begun at that point. As it was, she had some reservations about the financial and time commitment for the twice-a-week therapy, which she did begin.

The quality of her participation, the elaboration of more of her longstanding symptoms and problems with relationships, and his increasing grasp of the difficulties of her development and underlying conflicts convinced the analyst of both her need for, and her ability to succeed in, analysis. In only the third session, he questioned if the sense of power and control she felt in sexual relations might relate to an early experience of lack of control; she associated to an old dream going back to the time at age two or three when she and her parents lived in a trailer: an old man walked in, sat in the rocker a few minutes, and then walked out. She felt in telling this a sensation at the top of her head and back of her neck, had a sense of longing, and felt anxious and tearful. This was an early striking instance for the analyst that current puzzling emotion and behavior were connected with earlier and perhaps accessible roots.

Because she spoke freely, some of the details of her sexual fantasies suggested the likelihood of longstanding underlying intrapsychic conflicts. She felt the relationship with her man friend involved her "dark side" as against her more responsible, better self. She spoke of her intolerance for anger or disapproval. She showed ability to acknowledge apprehension about the analyst's reaction—that he must be critical of her not standing on her own feet—but then recognized this idea as possibly coming chiefly from herself.

Finally, after about ten weeks of treatment, the analyst was most impressed by a session in which she entered depressed after returning from a trip. She had gone to meet Bill at his urging, and he had been out temporarily. She related other memories of being left stranded, but when the analyst encouraged her to focus on the feeling she described of being alone, she remembered vividly coming home from school at age five and finding no one there. She ended the session tearful and reported next time that she had felt much better afterward.

Two weeks later her man friend began pressing her to renew the relationship. She felt drawn to him but also thought it would be destructive. His clear acknowledgment that he would not want children and would probably lose interest in her if she became pregnant finally broke her interest in him. However, she asked the analyst how to deal with the recurrent attraction. He almost apologetically replied that he thought she would need analysis. Then ensued two weeks of questioning what it was and would entail. When she spoke of how she wishes to be good but is afraid she will be bad, he said rather forcefully that she is immature and needs a chance to play. She, somewhat to his surprise, reflected on how she is always seen as mature. She wondered if maturity would mean resolving her concern and if she might attain it by analysis. He said he thought she might not be able to resolve all her questions about analysis in advance; the best way might be to try it. She asked if she could start at the next session. He said that they would have to arrange the additional times at the start of the session, but that then they could proceed.

In the next session, after the agreement to increase to three times a week, with the fourth session to begin the following month when a suitable time would be open, she said she felt she should have been angry at what he said of her immaturity, but instead she was excited. She had dreamed she was "going to do something bad, not in control, and didn't want to do it." Lying down she felt less able to fight. The analyst pointed out that sometimes people fought with others who stood for parts of themselves; and that analysis might help her get clearer about conflicts between different parts of herself and begin to master them.

In the opening phase of the analysis, she has continued to talk freely about feelings while increasingly reporting dreams and associations, memories, strong reactions to things she reads or sees or to encounters with people, and reactions to the analyst and her sense of his reactions. In relation to the couch, she expressed anger at her sense that she was naked while the analyst is dressed. When she moved from three to four times per week, she again questioned if she needed it or if he had just recommended it for the money. After saying this, she became tearful at her accusation; she feared conflict with him. She had set up a timetable for improvement which they linked with her fear of lack of control. As she realized increasing dependency on her sessions, she became tearful at feeling helpless, but was relieved by the analyst's distinguishing the feeling from actually being helpless and dependent. She moved from an anxious fantasy that it would not work with Bill to increasing attachment with him.

Meanwhile, however, the further emergence of phobic symptoms and longstanding depressive feelings allowed increasing acknowledgment of her need for the analysis even though the presenting issue of the relationship with Bill seemed less acute. She increasingly revealed fears of inadequacy as a woman, as a possible mother, and even as a professional when it came to taking responsibility for major decisions. She acknowledged concern and fantasies about the analyst's reactions and attitudes toward her. In terms of countertransference, the analyst moved during the therapy from responding to a certain titillating seductive quality to seeing her more as needing him in a parental way. Presenting analysis as a trial at first left him apprehensive at times lest she at some point stop prematurely; but he also saw this as a possibly a counteridentification with the patient's fears of abandonment.

The case report contains responses to the first four questions, though the final outcome is still undetermined. The decision to undertake psychotherapy and not psychoanalysis at the outset developed from several considerations: (a) what the patient wanted, that is, immediate help with current situations involving her new suitor and her motivation toward career or family: (the analyst had been recommended as a competent helper for emotional problems, not specifically because he could offer analysis); (b) the patient's character resistance, with an ideal of self-sufficiency and shame about dependency that would have probably prevented her from accepting an initial recommendation of analysis; (c) the analyst's concerns about the nature of her psychopathology, especially her impulsivity and distrust, perhaps relating to early separations from her mother, and doubts about her capacity to delay action in favor of fantasy and self-observation; (d) the analyst's belief, based on both theory and experience, that psychotherapy does not foreclose a shift to analysis, but by clarifying the depth, duration, and pervasiveness of problems allows both patient and analyst to be convinced of the need for it with a resulting more stable working alliance.

In response to our second question we would say, though the patient sat facing the analyst, the technique during psychotherapy otherwise differed little from the technique during analysis. Consonant with the outset of any treatment, the analyst provided orientation by suggesting she report what came to mind and look further at emotional conflicts underlying questions and problems with decision making. In therapy as in analysis, the analyst confronted contradictions, clarified especially her conflicting wishes and fears, and worked toward interpretation linking current dispositions to past experience. For example, the analyst related the gratification of feeling powerful and in control during sexual experience with an early experience of lack of control. The only advice given was to suggest that analysis would better help the patient achieve her emerging wishes for more insight and integration.

The decision to change from psychotherapy to psychoanalysis, our third question, developed from an increasingly clear connection of the manifest adult developmental issues around object choice and career with longstanding underlying anxiety, especially around separation, and unstable self-esteem. Furthermore, the patient showed both the capacity and disposition to use an analytic process, with emergence of affectively salient associations in response to interpretations and clarifications and with actual symptomatic relief from such meaningful connections of present and past. She also showed the capacity to distinguish her apprehension about the analyst's responses—for example, his disapproval—from the actuality. The timing of the change was related to the patient's increasing awareness of her needs correlated with recognizing the impossibility of a solution via her former lover. The increased trust in the analyst that developed during psychotherapy allowed her to appreciate the analyst's grasp of her immaturity as an alternative to her own sense of being bad.

The experience of the previous psychotherapy with its emerging alliance seemed to facilitate an opening phase in which the patient was very open about fears and fantasies, for example, fears in her dream of doing "something bad" or being "not in control," feelings on the couch of being less able to fight, or the idea the analyst was motivated to the shift by money lust. She indeed did seem generally more free in associating after the shift, including associating to words and images made out from the dots in the ceiling tiles. She also finally told the name of her former lover along with more about her feelings about that and other names.

The outcome—the effect of the total experience—is not yet known. Without preparatory psychotherapy, however, analysis would probably not have been undertaken.

Discussion

We believe that we have illustrated the usefulness of our questions for evaluating whether a shift from psychotherapy to psychoanalysis with the same analyst affected the process positively or negatively. Conditions in this case were such that neither patient nor analyst would have been comfortably able to undertake an analysis without the previous psychotherapy, which served as a useful preparation from the standpoint of both analyst and patient. Naturally many cases would have to be examined to assure that the questions provide an outline with broad applicability and that the answers come down one way or the other on the issue of the value of shifting.

We have tried to be empirical and atheoretical in our approach. Inevitably, the theory that analysts hold will shape their approach to their patients and their responses to our questions. Analysts who assume that the central feature of the treatment lies in the analysis of free associations minimally influenced by external cues, for example, will be exquisitely sensitive to possible compromises of neutrality, abstinence, and revelation of knowledge of the analyst. All are seen as potential contaminants to the spontaneous emergence and unmasking of unconscious structures and contents.

In contrast, analysts who assume the central feature of the treatment lies in the exploration of object-related transferences will regard the psychotherapy as an opportunity to form and observe transference phenomena. The subsequent analysis will be seen extending and expanding the exploration of already formed but now deepening transferences. Cautions that might interest the first group of analysts will seem to the second analytic group less significant.

Within any group many issues will receive more or less emphasis: How much compliance on the patient's part was demanded by the decision for therapy or analysis? Does the patient evidence an inclination toward loss of self-intactness? If the patient's self cohesion is fragile, how easily does restoration occur? Does the patient evidence psychological-mindedness, that is, an ease in processing introspective and interpretative information?

Let us return to Sally M and note in sequence what the analyst selected to report. First he offered an impression of the patient's motivation, giving the reader the impression that she was serious in her desire for help. Second he indicated his interest in her capacity for reality testing in making his decision about the choice of treatment. Next he offered an appraisal of her object relations and noted indications of both early and oedipal trauma. He then gave details of three patterns he discerned from her history. In one he noted a pathological repetition of her failure in relations with men. He stressed that she was consciously aware of her pattern and feared she would repeat it. In a second pattern, he described her adaptive repetition of intellectual and occupational success. In a third, he noted experiences of separation, fears of abandonment, and clinging dependent behavior. He noted that her immediate goal was to obtain help in making a decision. He expressed his concerns in opposites: was her problem essentially situational and therefore not requiring analysis? Did her characterological difficulties—her suspiciousness and a possible intolerance to experiencing affects without resort to action—preclude analysis? He was impressed that she took up his comment about her immaturity, dreamt about it, and worked with it.

We can conclude from his review that the case report reveals the nature of the analyst's concerns and his way of thinking about them—especially in terms of ego functional strengths and possible weaknesses. Another analyst might catalogue his approach more in terms of drives, yet another in terms of self state. We will nonetheless be able to discern the analyst's point of view; but, from this type of rendering, can we discern the patient's? It seems natural that analysts in describing their cases will reveal their concerns and what they experience. Yet to evaluate more fully and effectively how preliminary psychotherapy affects the later analysis, we need the patient's experience as well. More and more we have become sensitive to the issue of "fit" between analyst and patient, but have as yet only limited means of studying subtle intuitive impressionistic experiences. Clinical findings from analyses after shifting might be useful if the patient's experience is noted and reported.

An example comes from a protocol prepared for a conference on our subject by Dr. Becquer Benalcazar.

Mrs. J: I do not trust men. They cannot be honest. They never tell you what they like or dislike about you.

Dr. B: What is it that I don't like about you?

Mrs. J: What I remember of therapy is that you were more concrete. Analysis seems to be much more abstract.

Probably you were more practical in psychotherapy. In therapy I am sure you used to answer my questions. I remember, though, telling you a lot of my dreams. I know that was what I was supposed to do in therapy. But in analysis I do not know what to do.

Dr. B: I wonder if you are not getting ready to share with me some aspects about yourself that you did not feel you could share with me in therapy, and you want to make sure that I can take it.

Mrs. J: Yes, my father always got very shaky with me, as if he couldn't tolerate what I had to tell him.

Dr. B: Well, you see, instead of me giving you guidelines, you and I can ask what gets in the way of you letting me know what goes on in your mind. I wonder if you are seeing me as a punitive principle [her father] or as a shaky principal who can't take it.

Mrs. J: Well, you're right. But I think it is time for me to leave.

Dr. B: Yes, we should stop for now.

For the next two or three hours, Mrs. J complains of her passive silent father who did not talk to her and who maintained a distant style of relating.

This type of illustrative verbatim exchange added to case discussions provides invaluable additional information. The exchange reveals the patient during the opening phase of analysis describing her subjective appraisal of the difference between her experience during psychotherapy and analysis. It illustrates the way she weaves these experiences together with her past. Moreover, it documents a type of working together, a "fit," a sensitivity to one another, that draws on their mutual experience during psychotherapy.

1616 18th Street NW
Washington, DC 20009

Motivation for Psychoanalysis and the Transition from Psychotherapy

STEPHEN B. BERNSTEIN, M.D.

THE MOTIVATION NECESSARY FOR A PATIENT to accept the recommendation to enter psychoanalysis depends on a sufficient, ongoing level of distress experienced as internal, and the capacity to view an analyst as psychically safe and analysis as potentially leading to relief. In this paper I focus on the appropriate role of the analyst as psychotherapist in fostering such motivation and the process of its evolution.

Some factors that tend to foster the motivation for psychoanalysis include knowledge of its availability and potential benefits; an accepting external environment to support its conduct; the awareness that one's responses to external stresses are related to longstanding internal neurotic distress; and some experience of temporary relief and controllable regression obtained with an interested consultant, psychotherapist, or psychoanalyst.

The experienced clinician will recognize the process I describe as one that naturally involves establishing a treatment environment in which the patient's awareness is focused on his internal experience and conflict, and in which he can experience a safe and reversible regression. In this treatment environment the patient's motivation for analysis can be assessed and resistances to analysis can be voiced and explored. In some cases where these resistances

---

Dr. Bernstein is Training and Supervising Analyst, Boston Psychoanalytic Society and Institute, and Associate Clinical Professor of Psychiatry, Tufts University School of Medicine.

are more superficial, the exploratory process of an extended consultation may cause their sufficient modification and attentuation (they are raised to the level of awareness without working through) to allow the undertaking of an analysis.

In other cases analysis may represent a too sudden immersion in the unconsciously dangerous fantasy material, which may lead to a strong reluctance to enter analysis. The reluctance may be expressed as concerns about time, money, limitations imposed by occupation or other activities, or as a concern about "making treatment too important in my life." Here, a less intense form of treatment may be undertaken to allow the patient to have a more positive and controlled therapeutic experience and to explore and partially analyze the resistances to analysis. Such exploration may show that analysis has represented "the facilitator of a feared regression and the rekindling and reactivation of warded-off libidinal and aggressive impulses and wishes, which are experienced as more controllable in psychotherapy. In these patients, the recommendation for analysis stimulates regressive preexisting conflicts related to loss of control, isolation, deprivation, or object loss on the couch. Anxiety and regressive wishes are evoked and transference fantasies related to oral, anal, homosexual, phallic-oedipal, or genital wishes are activated toward the potential analyst" (Bernstein, 1983, p. 366). In addition, when a preparatory therapy is done by the same person who will continue as the analyst, this consistent observer can readily observe the progressive development of motivation and the analyst's role in fostering it.

Only recently has the "conversion" of psychotherapy to psychoanalysis been discussed in the literature (Horwitz, 1978; Bernstein, 1983; Gediman, 1984; Levine, 1985; Panel, 1987; Gill, 1988), because of questions about the compatibility of psychotherapy and psychoanalysis when they are conducted by the same analyst. Furthermore, as I have described elsewhere (1983) the issue of motivation for or reluctance to enter analysis has not been emphasized because of an initial need to clarify the definitions, boundaries, and compatibility of psychotherapy and psychoanalysis, and the meanings and effects of a previous psychotherapy on the transition and a subsequent psychoanalysis.

The continual need for writers to address the definitions and compatibility of therapy and analysis with the same analyst has been based on a longstanding attitude shaped by a confusing array of terms subject to linguistic and contextual influences and historical coloring. *Linguistically,* the term *psychotherapy* implies a unitary concept that an agreed-upon process, which is not in fact the case. The term *conversion* also has meanings relating to religion and even alchemy. *Contextually,* when comparing therapy and analysis, subtle changes in meaning occur in relation to clinical, theoretical, social, or political levels of observation. Clinically, for example, the level of observation may imperceptibly shift between types of interventions employed; techniques and boundaries of therapy; patient populations; and goals, curative agents, and outcomes (Wallerstein, 1969). And finally, *historically,* in order to differentiate psychoanalysis and protect it from confusion with the then current hypnotic therapies to which the term psychotherapy applied, Freud (1919) sharply distinguished between psychoanalysis and psychotherapy. Even though an analytically based psychotherapy now exists, some confusion resulting from the prior historical necessity still remains. Gediman (1984) has pointed out that some recent definitions of psychotherapy and psychoanalysis predefine differences between their processes, with therapy viewed as attempting to limit or not focus on a regressive transference. Here, the construction of the definition, not the observation of a clinical process, sets conditions that may cast doubt on the feasibility of the transition from psychotherapy to psychoanalysis. This is not the case with Gill (1988), who sees no such problem, since the psychoanalyst "should always be practicing psychoanalysis." Kris (1982) has also taken a useful approach that by-passes difficulties with definitions based on specific theories. Kris uses the concept of free association to relate therapy and analysis in terms compatible with a number of different theoretical approaches.

Evaluation of the patient's analyzability and motivation for analysis will usually occur in a consultation, an extended evaluation, or during an ongoing psychotherapy. In a consultation, the patient's need and readiness for analysis is assessed, and motivation may be fostered by demonstration, clarification, and interpretation of the underlying fears about analysis. An extension of the evaluation should occur only if the consultant is willing and able to continue in treatment with the patient because, after a few interviews, aspects of a therapeutic relationship may develop, and the consultant may come to play a significant role in the patient's psychic life. This development may greatly complicate the transference neurosis with a subsequent analyst (Hurst, 1980).

Some analysts think that, once the need for analysis has been ascertained and recommended, they are not able to continue with the patient in a less definitive treatment situation; they refer the patient to another therapist for therapy. It is my belief that with the maintenance of an analytic attitude in the therapy, and the anticipation of a possible transition to analysis, a more flexible position may be taken. The psychotherapy may continue as such, or there may be a transition to psychoanalysis. The actual type of treatment will arise from the developing therapeutic process and the capacities of the patient. Since a transition to analysis with the same analyst has been shown to have no untoward effects on the analysis (Bernstein, 1983; Levine, 1985; Horwitz in Panel [1987]) the preparatory therapy may now be seen in some instances to be part of the analysis or the opening phase of the analysis (Levine, 1985).

The patient's reluctance or lack of readiness to enter analysis may be related to several factors. (1) External situations or life turmoil may divert introspection and allow the patient to avoid experiencing his problems as internal. Here, analytic capacities may be submerged by superimposed responses to current stresses. The therapy may, for example, help the patient gain distance and a sense of control over previously preoccupying marital strife, occupational concerns, or issues of loss or mourning. Increased understanding of the meanings, repetitive nature, and underlying conflicts stirred by the current situation may help to detoxify and neutralize them, allowing a freeing up of emotional energy and making the patient's analyzability more evident (Gediman, 1984). (2) Intrapsychic distress may be experienced as overwhelming and may require some lessening in order for the patient to be able to fully participate in the analysis—the therapy brings about changes that make analysis possible. This may also be the case when certain more primitive developmental deficits become amenable to analytic change in the course of an ongoing therapeutic relationship (Rappaport, 1960; Shuren, 1967). And finally, (3) many seemingly analyzable patients are reluctant to enter analysis because the specific meaning of analysis to them is as a facilitator of regression which they think will be more controllable in psychotherapy. Preparatory therapy may sufficiently modify these fears to a level that will allow a transition to an analysis.

In each of these situations, the patient's wishes for a less intense form of treatment should be respected and a treatment context agreed upon in which external stresses, overwhelming anxiety, or fears of dependency and regression can be overtly addressed. The insistence that analysis is the only answer, or is all that will be offered, may force compliance or submission and is a poor way to begin a treatment. The suggestion that the patient see a consultant about his or her disagreement with the recommendation for analysis is useful only if there is a real question, and not in order to support one's recommendation by an appeal to authority. In therapy, however, an environment akin to that in analysis may be established and a process of exploration begun. The patient and analyst may continue to be interested in the patient's negative reaction to the idea of analysis and to explore its deeper meanings. A psychoanalytic context regarding the reasons for and demands of analysis may be gained, as well as an awareness of the degree to which the patient's life has been restricted as a result of his psychopathology (Bernstein, 1983). When treatment has begun in this way, patient and therapist have a common history of success in their work. The question of the recommendation for transition to analysis comes later in treatment, against the backdrop of a now more stable therapeutic alliance, a more evolved positive transference, a negative transference that has been modulated, and resistances that may have been partially analyzed.

The use of analytic psychotherapy as a trial of treatment is compatible with Freud's early (1913) recommendation of a trial of analysis for the evaluation of the patient's capacities and willingness for analysis. The large number of variables that affect analyzability and motivation are not easily predictable, however, in the one- or two-week time-limited trial period Freud described. Such a probationary phase is not generally used (Glover, 1955) because the appearance of deficits that would affect the analytic process may arise only after months or perhaps years (Greenson, 1967). Such a procedure may also put undue pressure on the patient, causing either compliance or withholding in the initial productions and thus leading to an inaccurate picture (Dewald, 1969). The implication of Freud's recommendation that only observation of the patient's functioning in the analytic situation can produce an accurate assessment of analyzability continues to be true. The analyst will always begin an analysis with an unstated sense of trial and exploration in relation to the patient's present and progressing capacities, and this stance will continue throughout the "analytic journey." Furthermore, for those patients with whom analysis is not initially possible because of reluctance or lack of preparedness, an analytic psychotherapy may allow a slower and more gradual introduction to treatment and serve as a useful approximation of the aims that Freud attempted to achieve by a trial of analysis.

The case of a stressed and anxious young law school graduate illustrates how a psychotherapy helped the capacity for analysis to reemerge, diminished reluctance to enter analysis, and then permitted transition. The patient had moved from another city to begin work four months before his wife, because of her previous professional commitments, could join him. Soon after beginning work, he began to feel anxious, had some difficulty concentrating at his office, and felt burdened by self-doubt and a sense of isolation. He was also bothered by some fantasies of a brief homosexual relationship five years before. This previously stable, well-functioning, sensitive, and psychologically-minded young man, whose character structure seemed well within the neurotic realm, recognized these current feelings and thoughts as alien.

Although the patient's emotional crisis initially required a therapeutic focus, his capacity to be analyzed was observed to reemerge over a six-month, once-a-week psychotherapy in which he was able to explore some of the determinants that underlay his current turmoil. These included the separation from his wife, as it repeated a childhood separation from his mother during her brief hospitalization, and concerns about competing at his first job. Decrease in his anxiety and some curiosity about the repetitive nature of his discomfort with competition eventually allowed the need for analysis to be broached. However, a strong reluctance to enter analysis now surfaced. Over the next year this was explored and understood in relation to longstanding fears about passivity and dependence and to issues concerning the unmourned loss of his father who had died when the patient was 15. His father was still vivid in his fantasies, and analysis threatened to revive the intense experience of guilt, anger, and loss from which he felt insulated. His father had been a lawyer whom he felt he was replacing. The process of mourning begun during the therapy allowed him to feel a new sense of relief and safety in the therapy. This fostered the initial positive transference and stable therapeutic alliance. With less need to defend against the intense feelings about his father's loss, the meanings of analytic treatment could be more easily explored. A transition to analysis eventually occurred.

Fostering the Development of Motivation

The therapeutic process leading to the modification of resistances to and motivation for undertaking psychoanalysis occurs on several different levels simultaneously. In what follows I describe the various components of this process. I should like to emphasize, however, that these components do not occur in sequence, even if it is necessary to present them that way.

Influence of the Recommendation of Analysis

The first component is the patient's awareness of the analyst's recommendation of psychoanalysis. This recommendation, although often anticipated by the patient, may be made by the analyst either during the initial evaluation or during the course of an ongoing therapy. A therapy in which the patient's reluctance to undertake analysis is an issue will be influenced in several ways. (1) The therapist will have made a specific recommendation, and the resistances to this will have been expressed early and may act as a focus. (2) Awareness of the possibility for transition may allow for the conduct of a treatment with a technical stance similar to that of the opening phase of an analysis, a stance that will not distort or interfere with the evolution of an unmodified analytic transference. (3) The patient experiences the topic of psychoanalysis as "in the air," and thus may experience reluctance as an overt disagreement with the therapist, which may cause reverberations in the subsequent therapy or analysis. (4) The ongoing issue of the reluctance as a microcosm of lifelong conflicts provides a shared frame of reference and may lead to a growing therapeutic alliance.

Some technical and practical issues related to the analyst's recommendation need to be mentioned. The way that analysis is recommended is significant, and may convey a message to the patient. I have heard presentations where the tentativeness of the recommendation reveals an underlying doubt about the usefulness of analysis or about the analyst's motive for suggesting it. Such a tentative recommendation as "Would you consider the possibility of a psychoanalysis" conveys a more ambivalent message than the straightforward assessment of needs observed and the reasons for the recommendation. This hesitancy may continue in the analyst's failure to interpret the patient's resistance to analysis as similar to issues of commitment to relationships, fears of intimacy, or sexual and aggressive inhibition which the patient has seen as repetitive conflicts in his life. The analyst's own questions about analysis and a resulting defensiveness may lead to a desire to convince the patient rather than to analytically understand an area of resistance. This ambivalence about the recommendation may lead to a countertransference inhibition and avoidance of the subject of analysis, manifest as fears of manipulating, seducing, or "selling" the patient on analysis.

Bassen (1989) has described situations in which the recommendation for analysis resulted from a multidetermined interaction of appropriate clinical indications for analysis, the patient's transference needs for certain responses from the therapist, and corresponding needs in the potential analyst. The patient's need for actualization of the transference wishes (such as wishes to change passively, to thwart the therapist, or to disavow feelings) may evoke countertransference actions in the therapist (such as the desire to do more for the patient or make the patient change). The countertransference may become actualized in the recommendation for beginning an analysis or for the conversion of a therapy to an analysis. Bassen believes that the vulnerability to the transference-countertransference enactments in which she feels she has participated in the cases she cites were the result of unresolved neurotic difficulties, specific meanings that being a candidate in analytic training had for her, and the concurrent need to find cases suitable for training, and "the fairly universal wish of analysts to do more analysis."

The timing and decision to recommend analysis may be a response to evoked feelings of impotence or incompetence when the patient has expressed hopelessness, dissatisfaction, or urgency in the therapy; when the patient has disavowed needs and affects and leaves these to be experienced only by the therapist; or when a withholding or oppositional patient has expressed concern about ever changing. The therapist may want to use the most "powerful" treatment to counter the patient's fears and allay his own doubts about his capacities or effectiveness. If the therapist is further vulnerable because of needing the patient, for example, to fulfill a training requirement, the therapist may be less able to step back from the investment in the recommendation to examine the transference manifestations that are pressing for actualization. Bassen points out that neither inexperience nor the intensity of an ongoing treatment relationship alone can account for the situations she described. In one case an analytic supervisor felt that the recommendation was clinically indicated. In another case a senior consultant referred a patient to her for analysis after having recommended analysis to the patient. This patient felt unprepared for and upset by the recommendation and felt she had no choice in the type or frequency of treatment. Bassen, unaware of this at the time and eager to find an analytic patient, thought the patient had agreed with the recommendation. Bassen feels the patient unconsciously engineered the transference-countertransference enactment with both the consultant and the potential analyst around the recommendation for analysis.

The process of transference pressure and countertransference need, such as can occur in relation to the recommendation for analysis, may influence many other interactions in the course of therapy or analysis. The analyst's unexamined need for the patient may affect his clinical judgment and distort his evaluation of the patient's analyzability. It may lead to a precipitate onset of analysis, or it may underlie a failure to anticipate ego regression and cause a delay in the use of ego-supportive measures in certain patients. Moreover, the analyst may react against the unconscious need for the patient by the previously mentioned fears of selling the patient on analysis or seducing the patient into analysis. Such reaction formations may account for some of the analyst's ambivalence about analysis and its recommendation.

The countertransference needs described make it technically difficult to pursue the negative aspects of a specific conflict, such as the "wish not to be in analysis." The analyst's need for the patient may result in a subtle avoidance of certain negative transference issues, a tendency to deflect and displace away from the transference to the outside, or a narrowing of the focus of the process, as well as influencing the recommendation for analysis. However, it may be that some of these countertransference responses can be seen only in retrospect. The analyst's relative vulnerability to manifesting them may vary at specific times. The effect of these responses on the analysis may also depend on the defensive organization of the patient, the state of the therapeutic alliance, and the phase of the analysis.

Some practical conditions do exist for the patient and analyst. Time and cost may be real issues. Out of a wish to do a certain amount of analysis, the analyst may choose to reduce his fee somewhat for analysis. A flexible ability in the analyst to occasionally adjust the appointment times may be useful for certain patients, such as the lawyer who is unexpectedly called to court, the medical resident on call, or the graduate student during an examination period. The fact that such a reduction of fee or time flexibility may also serve the patient's resistance and will affect the patient's transference fantasies must obviously be kept in mind.

An Internal Locus of Distress

Meanwhile the analyst is turning his attention to the patient's use of externalization to defend against the internal source of his or her neurotic distress. Persistent preoccupation with external sources of conflict decreases motivation by deflecting internal distress. The patient asks the therapist to solve external situations or indirectly treat a spouse or other family member. Some ackowledgment of the external situation may be useful, but tactful interpretation of the preexisting and repetitive nature of the themes underlying the external situations, that they are "portable" and have been carried to different situations, and that they have preexisted current relationships helps to attenuate the defense, locate the distress and conflict internally, and thereby increase motivation for intrapsychic change.

An opera singer entered treatment because of marital strife with her husband, who seemed jealous of her increasing success in her career as compared with his own professional work. She complained frequently about his resenting the increased demands on her time. She had also noticed in herself a waning satisfaction with her singing and difficulties in getting herself to practice. During a one-year, twice-weekly psychotherapy, her sensitivity to her husband's demands were repeatedly seen and interpreted, in part, as an externalization of her preexisting guilt over her competitive strivings stirred by her current successes. She became less fixed on needing to prove to her therapist her husband's need to control her by her repetitive elaboration of his jealous comments. She began to see that her reaction had been present in her prior relationships. This led her to wonder about her reactions to her recent increased professional recognition.

Eventually, a reduction in the use of externalization allowed a greater sense of internal distress and motivation for a transition to analysis. It became increasingly clear in the analysis that her conflicts about her career were related to early envy of an older sister who had had a beautiful singing voice but who had died when the patient was ten. In fact, the patient's interest in singing began after her sister's death as an identification with her and as a way of replacing her. The patient became increasingly able to understand her competitive wishes as well as those of her husband in relation to her. She saw that some of her compliance with his wishes for her to limit her performances was rooted in guilt related to her competitive wishes toward her sister. Her competitive wishes also stirred her husband. Deepening insight allowed the patient to feel less dominated by his demands and also allowed her to be able to more deeply appreciate and support his own outstanding professional capacities.

This patient's life situation had in part been used as a defense against awareness of inner conflict. Although she had previously been analyzable, her use of externalization as a defense against awareness of conflicts related to envy, guilt, competition, and mourning had led her to focus attention away from an experience of internal distress.

Recognition of Limitations Caused by Neurotic Miseries

A third component of the process I am describing is the analyst's demonstration and the patient's sustained recognition that the patient's neurotic miseries have led to limitations in a wide area of functioning. Limitations in various areas of the patient's life may not be fully apparent to him and may require "some preparatory psychotherapy in order to lead the patient to the realization that he needs a more radical therapy" (Greenson, 1967, p. 359). A patient's complaint that he cannot "open up" or say what he feels to a loved one may be shown by the therapist to extend to other significant areas of the patient's life, for example, the businessman's difficulty in communicating with his boss, the graduate student's inhibition in writing a doctoral dissertation, or the salesman's fears of calling his customers. By clarification of the sources and nature of the frustration, inhibition, dysfunction, and painful affects, the patient gains understanding of the extent to which he has been limited, and the means, methods, and possibility of change. A patient who tended to minimize the effect of his neurotic conflicts and saw his difficulties as being limited to his marriage because of his wife's demands for attention and feelings that he was, at times, critical and devaluing, was helped to see that these were similar to complaints by women colleagues in his professional office, as well as in numerous past relationships. The eventual acknowledgment of the difficulties as internal, preexisting, and carried throughout his life, allowed the patient to search for the severe limitations these had caused in personal and professional areas of his life, and to explore the restrictions as they later became manifest in the analytic transference.

The Parallel of Fears in Life and Fears in Treatment

Concomitant with the foregoing component of the process of fostering motivation for psychoanalysis is the patient's recognition of the parallel between his fears outside the treatment and his fears in treatment. When the patient becomes aware of the extent to which internal conflicts produce limitations in his life, he may be helped to see the extent of the limitations he imposes on the treatment, which are also a result of these conflicts. The resistance to analysis may be seen as a microcosm of his underlying difficulties. Fears of commitment, dependency, intimacy, or competition in the treatment may be seen to have a common origin and a common hope of alleviation. Thus the transference can be seen as similar to manifestations of both internal and external distress, and perhaps as the medium of change. A patient whose conflicts related to intimacy, for example, had failed in several relationships with women but had recently fallen in love. One day he said with anxiety and pressure, "I see the signs of my old needs to withdraw and isolate myself creeping into my new relationship, in the same way I've seen them in my mistrust of my relationship with you. I just hope I can change them here so that they will change outside, before I mess up that relationship."

A businessman sought treatment because of difficulties in his marriage. His wife was extremely dissatisfied with their lack of intimacy and his emotional distance and preoccupation with his work. She was distressed by his ruminations and "making lists" about what he had to do at work, and knew this caused him "not to be there" at times. The patient felt he was being pushed into treatment, compelled to be a "good boy," and to comply with his wife's urgency that he change. In a twice-weekly therapy, he began to see his anxiety, ruminations, distance in relationships, and need to comply as lifelong preoccupations related to all-encompassing family expectations for achievement in all areas of his early life. The patient was strongly motivated against analysis. And yet analysis seemed to be the only way this man could be adequately freed from severe guilt and inhibitions. His reluctance was seen to be related to fears of revealing his underlying rebelliousness and rage, which he defended against by compliance, distance, and obsessional preoccupations. The patient gradually became aware of his withdrawal in the therapy and his flight to the "lists" of what he had to do after the session. These "flights" from me he saw as typical interruptions. He saw that the ruminations occurred at specific times, drew us away from certain charged areas and toward other areas, were related to an affective distancing, and also stirred in him a sense of guilt at not doing the "right thing."

The ruminations served as a "marker" of areas to be avoided, and of feelings and fantasies that might be approaching the surface. They also helped to maintain distance from the regressive intimacy the patient was beginning to experience. The re-creation and then the interpretation of the symptoms in the transference allowed him to see the parallel between the limitations in his life and in the treatment relationship. This insight brought the resistance to analysis into clearer focus.

Some Comfort With Analytic Regression

Many patients experience analysis as the potential facilitator of feared and uncontrolled regression. When patients in psychotherapy give evidence of experiencing comfort in controlled regression, the therapist may sense that they are in a state of readiness for transition to psychoanalysis. This comfort may be noted in various ways. The patient may spend more time in a relaxed, somewhat recumbent position in the chair and look away while associating, relying less on the therapist's facial and verbal responses. At meaningful moments, the patient may glance furtively at the couch. The material tends to be more open, and the issue of analysis is more easily raised by either patient or therapist. The patient may spend more time thinking about the treatment and acknowledge fantasied discussions with the therapist during the time between meetings. Such increased motivation for analysis was apparent in the "slip" of a patient in once-weekly psychotherapy: "I want to talk about this tomorrow, I mean next week." The therapist also senses less resistance as an increased timelessness in the hour, less need to intervene, and a greater capacity for free-floating attention. He may also experience in himself a sense of greater calm and less physical tension at times of the patient's reduced resistance. The therapist sometimes has the inner experience of an ongoing process similar to that experienced while doing analysis.

With greater motivation for analysis, dreams may be more frequent, associations may seem richer, and their themes may show more tolerance for regression. Such dreams have expressed themes of going on a trip with someone or going back to an earlier time. They may also depict going downward, which in part relates to a greater tolerance for the regressive experience. A patient at an advanced state of readiness for analysis dreamed that she was on a hill looking down into a valley below where her family was having an enjoyable picnic. She wanted to go down and join them, but was not sure how to get there. She had the choice of rolling down a steep incline in what she feared would be an uncontrolled manner or taking an old "rickety" elevator. The elevator seemed safer, but might stop and not get there and had its own potential dangers. She explored the dream as relating to her choice between continuing in the therapy, which had been useful but in which she now saw limitations, and chancing what she envisioned as the less controllable "rolling down" of the analysis.

Certain patients seem to fear the analytic regression because they are concerned it will remove their control over a real or fantasied experience of loss. Where the history includes the early death of a parent or sibling, a continuing unmourned loss (Fleming, 1972, 1975) and an ongoing relationship in fantasy with the lost object may continue (Wolfenstein, 1969) and may need to be protected. Resumption of the mourning process and a willingness to begin giving up the illusion of a continuing relationship with the lost object may indicate a readiness for psychoanalysis.

We can learn much about the importance of the patient's comfort with an analytic regression by studying the group of patients who continue to avoid analysis and whose continued resistance seems related to a strong intolerance for such regression. At a certain point they limit their involvement in therapy and refuse to go further. Many of these patients seem to have certain characteristics in common. In general, throughout their lives they have relied heavily on strong counterdependent defenses and have had subtle narcissistic needs for distance. Although most seem even more analyzable than some other patients who have entered psychoanalysis, they have had difficulties with intimacy and are suspicious of whether the therapist is really interested in them. A number of these patients have needed to develop a precocious sense of self-reliance as a defense against frustrated dependency yearnings. As children, several were taken by their parents to live in foreign countries. Both parents and child felt some fear and confusion in their new surroundings, and the child was prematurely called upon to decipher a new language and culture. One patient was born in a foreign country soon after his parents had moved there. His parents never assimilated into the culture of the country, did not learn the language, and the child had to act as their interpreter. Another patient was the oldest female child in a family of ten and had to assume a caretaker role at a relatively young age. Others responded with "self-reliance" after the birth of a closely spaced younger sibling. Such patients may envision analysis as the fostering of a frustrating dependency or as the need to learn a "new language" in which they will be misunderstood.

These counterdependent patients may have an underlying mild depression, with a sense of hopelessness that they will ever be able to change substantially, in spite of evident symptomatic relief in the therapy. The continued visual contact seems necessary to protect against the feeling of being controlled and may have other specific genetic-dynamic meanings. Although the therapist may suspect an underlying ego-regressive potential, this seems not to be the case. These patients are not necessarily schizoid or paranoid, nor do they have other specific primitive characteristics. They are not, however, comfortable with states of relaxation, creative play, or pleasurable interpersonal regression. Masochistic trends may also be present, and they seem to have a level of unconscious guilt that they experience as threatening and constantly in need of control. Why these patients continue to avoid analysis, however, while others with similar presentations become motivated, still remains a question.

The daughter of a depressed, self-critical mother and a strong, ambitious, and demanding father illustrates some of these tendencies to counterdependent resistance and fears of dependency and regression. The patient had partial identifications with aspects of both parents. She had competitive feelings, tinged with guilt, toward an older sister, and a secret special relationship with her devaluing father, a relationship that he acknowledged mainly by smiling faintly in a special way in response to her overt demands for his approval of some achievement on her part. As she remembered it, he saw needs as weakness; only successes produced his approval. In therapy, this patient was cooperative and showed a capacity for gaining insight. Her resistance seemed to center on the fear of regression and what it might uncover. This fear became clearer to us both one day at the close of a particularly intense hour. The patient rose from her chair and started toward the door. As she neared the door she lost her balanced and tripped. She fell to one knee and remained there, sobbing, refusing help, for several minutes. She spoke of her utter humiliation at her "stupidity" and about the therapist seeing her in this weakened condition. Her fears about being seen as "weak" and dependent were now evident to both of us. It was apparent that she did not want to experience these feelings nor did she want me to see them. Because of this patient's conflicts, she titrated and controlled the time that she would allow to explore her resistances to a more intense treatment. Although substantial symptomatic change was apparent in areas of her marriage and career after four years of therapy, she chose to "live" with her mild to moderate depression, at least for the present. Transition to analysis did not occur. For the analyst to have pressed for a transition would have led to the evolution of a sadomasochistic transference struggle, a nonproductive stalemate, a negative therapeutic reaction, or perhaps an unanalyzable destructive struggle to regain visual contact for the purpose of counterdependent control.

Dissatisfaction with the Limitations of Psychotherapy and a Desire to Intensify the Treatment

A crucial factor in the motivation for analysis is that the patient may come to realize that in psychotherapy once or twice a week much of the time is taken up with the "crust" of resistance, which must be removed in each session, as well as the anticipation of leaving at the end of the hour. The conflicts can be demonstrated, but an ongoing and deepening process seems severely limited. Gradually, in response to the patient's realization of this, and its acknowledgment by the therapist, dissatisfaction with the limitations of the therapy may motivate the patient to increase his commitment to an expanded treatment. The patient may complain that the hour ends in the middle of the analysis of a dream, may wonder why he feels so "distant" after a week's separation, and may want to keep and sustain a new sense of interest or involvement at the end of the hour. The patient may note an increased freedom of associations during the middle of the hour as compared to the resistances at its beginning; or, when for some reason two hours have been scheduled close together in the week, he may notice an increased freedom in the second hour. The patient may begin to complain about feeling less progress in the treatment than he would like.

In response to a patient's growing dissatisfaction with the effects of his or her resistance, I occasionally try to clarify the forces at work by the use of various metaphors. I may mention how people keep their feelings and thoughts locked behind closed doors and that these keep some fears in check, but at the expense of restricting one's activity and life. I mention the possibility of exploring behind the closed doors in a more intense treatment. I have found this image and model of defense has led to deepening responses in a number of patients. One patient remembered a continuing fantasy soon after learning of his father's death when he was eight. He had returned home after spending a week at his grandmother's house because of his father's illness. On entering the house, he bounded upstairs to see his father. His mother said that he should not open his father's bedroom door but should instead come and talk with her. He opened the door and saw the room was empty. His mother then told him of his father's death. He told me of his continuing fantasy that if he had listened to his mother, and had not opened the door, his father would still be alive. Bitter at not having been told sooner of his father's illness and still angry at the loss, he had been trying to close and lock the door ever since. He was able to see the door as his need to control his unacceptable feelings and yearnings, for which he felt he had been and would be punished. He also saw his excessive need to control himself in relationships with women and in the therapy.

At other times, I use the metaphor of the patient and myself sitting in a boat, trying to look at some clouded image below the surface that we need to find some way to see more clearly. The patient understands that the distortion of the water is, in part, the resistance, and that greater clarity may come from increased intensity of observation. The use of such metaphors seems to objectify the internal struggle the patient is experiencing and to foster a joint and allied search, and is inspired by Freud's (1913, p. 135) description of free association to his patient through the image of "a traveller sitting next to the window of a railway carriage and describing to someone inside the carriage the changing views" seen outside.

Anticipation and Response to the Transition

The periods before and after the transition are a time for the analysis of fantasies about the transition, "loss" of the therapist and "gain" of a "new" analyst. A sense of separation, loss, deprivation, being controlled, and hope for greater involvement and interest may be anticipated before and experienced after the transition. Many of the factors Kris (1982) has described as sustaining an analysis the patient has also experienced in the therapy and anticipates continuing in the analysis. These factors include the conscious desire for the relief of symptoms and the need for change; the friendly interest and focus of attention of the analyst, with pleasure in the prospect of a joint venture; the experience of positive transference; and the hope engendered by all of these. In addition, Kris has mentioned the enormous satisfaction of feeling understood, the greater understanding of oneself, the excitement of growing insight, and the satisfaction in the activity of free association.

The immediate pre- and post-transition periods are also a time for examination of possible countertransference responses to the patient's transition. Countertransference responses, discussed earlier in connection with the recommendation for analysis, may continue with the transition to analysis. The analyst may be concerned that the transition is the result of compliance, seduction, some hidden destructive competition, or masochistic surrender. Awareness of the potential for these reactions is important, as is the potential use, when necessary, of consultative discussion about the clinical indications and appropriateness of the transition.

Finally, some important effects of the transition, which have been described elsewhere (Horwitz, 1978; Bernstein, 1983; Levine, 1985; Horwitz [Panel, 1982]) are: (1) a marked intensification of the therapeutic process; (2) an increase of early memories associated with freeing of affective expression; (3) a deepening of the already apparent early regressive transference; and, when it arises, (4) continued analysis of the therapy experience in the analysis.

Acknowledgment

I am grateful to Dr. David A. Berkowitz and Judith Bernstein for significant comments on this paper, and to Dr. Anton O. Kris for helpful comments on an earlier version.

REFERENCES

Bassen, C. (1989). Transference-countertransference enactment in the recommendation to convert psychotherapy to psychoanalysis.*Int. Rev. Psychoanal.*, 16:79–92.

Bernstein, S. B. (1983). Treatment preparatory to psychoanalysis. *J. Amer. Psychoanal. Assn.*, 31:363–390.

Dewald, P. A. (1969). *Psychotherapy: A Dynamic Approach*. New York: Basic Books.

Fleming, J. (1972). Early object deprivation and transference phenomena: The working alliance. *Psychoanal. Quart.*, 41:23–49.

______ (1975). Some observations on object constancy in the psychoanalysis of adults. *J. Amer. Psychoanal. Assn.*, 23:743–759.

Freud, S. (1913). On the beginning of treatment. *S.E.,* 12.

_____ (1919). Lines of advance in psycho-analytic therapy. *S.E.,* 17.

Gediman, H. K. (1984). On the transition from psychotherapy to psychoanalysis with the same analyst. Unpublished.

Gill, M. M. (1988). Converting psychotherapy into psychoanalysis. *Contemp. Psychoanal.,* 24:262–274.

Glover, E. (1955). *The Technique of Psycho-analysis.* New York: Int. Univ. Press.

Greenson, R. R. (1967). *The Technique and Practice of Psychoanalysis.* New York: Int. Univ. Press.

Horwitz, L. (1978). A comparison of psychoanalysis and psychotherapy with the same patient. Unpublished.

Hurst, D. M. (1980). Some Effects of the Consultation-Referral Process on Subsequent Analytic Work. *J. Amer. Psychoanal. Assn.,* 28:605–621.

Kris, A. O. (1982). *Free Association: Method and Process.* New Haven/London: Yale Univ. Press.

Levine, H. B. (1985). Psychotherapy as the initial phase of psychoanalysis. *Int. Rev. Psychoanal.,* 12:285–297.

Panel (1987). Conversion of Psychotherapy to Psychoanalysis, C. P. Fisher, Reporter. *J. Amer. Psychoanal. Assn.,* 35:713–726.

Rappaport, E. A. (1960). Preparation for analysis. *Int. J. Psychoanal.,* 41:626–632.

Shuren, I. (1967). A contribution to the metapsychology of the preanalytic patient. *Psychoanal. Study Child,* 22:103–136.

Wallerstein, R. S. (1969). The relationship of psychoanalysis to psychotherapy—current issues. *Int. J. Psychoanal.,* 50:117–126.

Wolfenstein, M. (1969). Loss, rage, and repetition. *Psychoanal. Study Child,* 24:432–460.

146 Wallis Road
Chestnut Hill, MA 02167

Psychotherapy as a Trial for Psychoanalysis

LEONARD HORWITZ, Ph.D.

A STRIKING PHENOMENON IN PSYCHOANALYTIC literature is the relatively scant coverage of a process to which psychoanalysts are paying increasing attention: converting psychotherapy to psychoanalysis with the same treater. Only two articles have appeared specifically addressed to this topic and both have been recent (Bernstein, 1983; Levine, 1985). The reasons for the dearth of material on this subject are not entirely clear, but may be related to the relative infrequency of the procedure in the past. The last major survey of psychoanalytic practice (conducted by the American Psychoanalytic Association in 1976 [Shapiro, 1980]) revealed that 12 percent of the patients then in psychoanalytic treatment had seen their analysts first in psychotherapy. In contrast, 40 percent of this patient pool had had previous psychotherapy with a different analyst.

The recent proliferation of workshops, panels, and articles on this topic indicates that the 12-percent figure may be considerably higher today. Since the early 1980s the American Psychoanalytic Association has sponsored several discussion group on the subject, including a panel in 1983 (Panel, 1987), suggesting that the process of converting is a subject of much greater interest than it was heretofore and is unquestionably regarded as a boon to candidates and graduate analysts seeking psychoanalytic cases.

Dr. Horwitz is Training and Supervising Analyst at the Topeka Institute of Psychoanalysis.

In this paper, I present an instance in which initial doubts about a patient's analyzability led to psychotherapy being used to assess the patient's suitability. What I am here referring to is a trial *for* analysis, rather than a trial analysis per se. Most analysts would agree that every psychoanalysis begins with a trial period, and if the patient is unable to tolerate the strain of the procedure or is unable to work productively, then treatment is switched to psychotherapy. This procedure is often followed when the indications for analysis outweigh the contraindications. On the other hand, when serious doubts exist about a patient's analyzability, but psychoanalysis has not been ruled out, analysts frequently begin once- or twice-a-week psychotherapy and then convert to analysis if the patient proves capable.

With these dubious cases, there is no real consensus on the desirability of beginning with analysis versus beginning with psychotherapy or vice versa. Many analysts adhere to Freud's recommendation (1913) that a trial period of analysis is desirable when in doubt, but we must remember that psychoanalytic psychotherapy as we currently know it was not available in those early days. The alternative to psychoanalysis proper at that time was a form of treatment incorporating suggestion, education, advice, and direct intervention. The so-called intermediate forms of treatment in which a relatively inactive therapist assumes a neutral role and interprets the transference have appeared on the scene only in the past few decades.

The argument in favor of a trial analysis, of course, is that it affords the clearest and most conclusive test of analyzability. However, those patients who are unable to pass the test must make a painful transition back to psychotherapy. They are often burdened by feelings of failure and guilt and in some cases must cope with iatrogenic regressive experiences that occurred while using the couch. Advantages of beginning with psychotherapy are that it may clarify diagnostic considerations and gives the analyst an opportunity to gauge the patient's capacity to use transference interpretations. If analysis is ruled out, psychotherapy may be continued without altering the structural arrangements of the treatment and without having to reduce its frequency, an even more difficult task.

An addititional point I hope to make is that it is possible that previous psychotherapy may serve to strengthen the patient's ego, thus permitting a psychoanalysis that might not otherwise have been possible. It would seem that we are exploring virgin territory here, since, to my knowledge, no one has yet written clearly and explicitly to this topic.

With regard to differentiating psychotherapy from psychoanalysis, Gill (Panel, 1987) has disavowed his earlier (1954) views and now maintains that only one criterion should be used, namely, the centrality of the analysis of the transference. He now believes that the use of the couch and the frequency of the sessions are "external criteria" and not absolutely essential. My own view accords with that of Kernberg (1982), who contends that these external criteria are basic to the analytic setting, necessary, but not sufficient, for a definition of psychoanalysis. That is, without the internal criterion of transference analysis, an analysis is not being conducted, whatever its external trappings.

Bernstein (1983) and Levine (1985) have described patients who required once-a-week psychotherapy lasting almost a year before they were motivated to invest the time and money required by psychoanalysis. In both instances, the patients were assessed as eminently analyzable, but their neurotic conflicts, as well as their lack of understanding of the psychoanalytic process, contributed to their unwillingness or unreadiness to become engaged in psychoanalysis.

Bernstein's patient was a young married woman whose fear of psychoanalysis was based on an unconscious fantasy that the analytic process would lead her to lose control of her temper and that her eruption of anger would cause the analyst to get rid of her, just as her biological parents had given her up for adoption immediately after her birth. In the preparatory psychotherapy, the analyst helped the patient understand why she feared a more intense process, and eventually the patient came to feel that psychoanalysis would actually contribute to an increased sense of control rather than the reverse. At the same time, she began to feel that more frequent appointments were necessary for her to achieve her goals. During the year-long preparatory phase, the analyst conducted expressive, exploratory psychotherapy and maintained a neutral position. After switching to analysis, the patient achieved a successful analytic result in three years.

Levine's patient was similar in many respects. She was a young married woman with chronic feelings of worthlessness and anxiety, episodes of overeating, and a fear of being abandoned by her husband because of her unattractiveness and sexual inhibitions. Although the analyst initially regarded her as analyzable, he believed that an immediate recommendation for analysis would have produced a negative reaction. "She had come expecting weekly therapy and the suggestion of a more intensive treatment might well have precipitated a degree of anxiety and opposition that she was not ready to examine" (p. 286). After ten months of once-a-week psychotherapy, the analyst decided that the patient's conflicts concerning her oedipal wishes and fears would require more intensive treatment. At the same time, the patient indicated a desire for more frequent sessions, so the analyst's recommendation for analysis was received quite positively. Levine concluded that his case illustrated a useful "alternative pathway to psychoanalysis or a variant of the opening phase. For patients such as the one presented here, an introductory psychotherapy phase may even be a necessary prerequisite if an analysis is to occur" (p. 296).

When Eissler (1953) introduced the concept of a parameter, which he defined as a departure from basic technique that is used when unmodified psychoanalysis will not suffice and is later undone or abolished by interpretation, he clearly implied that some form of ego strengthening or structure building must occur before conducting an unmodified psychoanalytic process.

G. Blanck and R. Blanck (1974) clearly believed that preparatory psychotherapy with patients who show ego deficits may, in some instances, bring the patients to the point where they are analyzable. "If early experiences, despite trauma, have provided a modicum of good-enough self and object representations, psychotherapy for structure building may lead to psychoanalysis after identity is established. These become very long-term cases, but if patient and therapist have the necessary endurance, their work together can be exceptionally rewarding" (p. 123). They described a patient who lacked a firm identity (particularly with regard to gender), who was convinced that the therapist had the capacity and the desire to read her mind, and who lacked firm repressive boundaries around oedipal wishes and fears. After several years of ego-building and the development of a firm therapeutic alliance, her treatment "took a more classical psychoanalytic form" (p. 125).

There appear to be three broad categories of patients who are started in psychotherapy and later considered for psychoanalysis. The first group consists of patients with either dubious indications or even definite contraindications for psychoanalysis. This category includes patients with serious ego defects or ego weaknesses—certain borderline and narcissistic patients, or patients with impulse disorders or addictive disorders. The second group consists of those patients for whom psychoanalysis is definitely indicated as the treatment of choice but must be excluded for reasons such as geographic distance, economic circumstances, external life conditions that preclude a long-term commitment, situational crises, such as a recent separation or divorce, or mourning after the death of a loved one. The third category of patients also includes those for whom psychoanalysis is the treatment of choice but who, because of neurotic conflicts often combined with a lack of sophistication about psychoanalysis, are unable to commit themselves to the required level of effort in time and money. This group includes patients who fear dependency, loss of autonomy, or commitment to an intense relationship. One might describe this reluctance and low motivation as a fear of exposing one's "hidden self," so effectively described by Bernstein (1983).

Case Example

The patient I am presenting fits principally into the first category of those who present questionable initial indications for psychoanalysis.

A 29-year-old married professional man was in expressive psychotherapy twice a week for two years and nine months. He sought analytic treatment for vaguely defined character problems, relating mainly to his tendency to be distant and overly inhibited in relationships. Described initially as passive-aggressive and masochistic, he presented as soft-spoken and reserved with marked obsessional features, and he tried to keep his options open as long as possible. His lifestyle was anhedonic, parsimonious, and cautious.

The patient requested analysis, but a previous diagnostic evaluation raised questions about his suitability. Perhaps the most important factor leading to doubt about analysis was the patient's traumatic early childhood. He was the youngest of four children, with three older sisters who ranged in age from 10 to 19 at the time of his birth. His father had died when he was two, and the patient initially had no recollections of him. His mother's mental stability was questionable even before her husband's death; thereafter she became increasingly paranoid and isolated from her family. During the next two to three years, the patient's sisters left home and he and his mother led a nomadic existence, moving from town to town as his mother frantically sought to elude her would-be persecutors and pursuers. Even when young, the patient was aware that his mother's thinking was disturbed and irrational, and he recalled feeling embarrassed when they were together in public. She often relied on him to help correct her distorted ideas and to restrain her from impulsive actions. To decrease the threat of being at the mercy of someone whose actions were dictated by paranoid distortions, the patient found it necessary to control and manipulate his mother. When he was five, his mother was hospitalized and he was adopted by an uncle and aunt.

In addition to this traumatic history, other features of the initial evaluation suggested ego weakness. The psychologist noted a "remoteness which would require an intrusive, vibrant presence" by the therapist to make sufficient contact with the patient. The consultant who evaluated the patient saw a blandness of affect that interfered with forming emotional rapport. Also, the patient himself reported hypnagogic experiences in his childhood that recurred in his adolescence: He saw the Virgin Mary wearing transparent clothes and, while seeing her thus exposed, he heard a roaring sound that came closer and closer. This experience first occurred around age four but returned when the patient was in his early twenties and struggling with important career and lifestyle decisions. This combination of a traumatic early history and certain equivocal signs of ego weakness disposed the evaluating team toward the more conservative recommendation of psychotherapy. Psychological testing also raised some cautions about analysis, based mainly on some "soft signs" of ego weakness that might require supportive parameters in a psychoanalytic process. But the recommendation of the tester was that to modify the patient's marked passive-aggressive and masochistic character, the intensive process of analysis was necessary.

The initial extensive workup included five psychiatric interviews with the patient, five interviews with his wife, one joint interview, and a full battery of psychological tests. In regard to the patient's history, the interviewer was impressed by the "scars of childhood" that this man must have suffered as a result of the serious traumas in the first five years of his life. In addition, the interviewer was concerned about the vivid hypnogogic experiences that involved "visions" of the Virgin Mary in the nude. In the examination itself, the interviewer worried about the patient's hyperobsessionalism and his rambling, circumstantial thinking. Furthermore, the patient's affect was constricted to the point of "blandness," most apparent in his flat way of talking about unusually stressful and chaotic periods of his life. The examiner found it difficult to make emotional contact with him. All these evidences of ego weakness gave rise to concern that the patient's rigid obsessive and compulsive defenses were vulnerable to further decompensation and that psychoanalysis could indeed induce increased regression.

The psychological testing also raised doubts about the integrity of the patient's ego. There were mild word misusages, tendencies on the Rorschach test to allow things to come together that do not go together in real life, a failure to give any whole human responses, as well as a dearth of popularly seen percepts. Consistent with the patient's uncomfortable feeling of emotional distance from others, the characters in his T.A.T. stories tended to be shallow, distant, and unrealized. The psychologist described his findings as "subtle but substantial evidence of a weakness in ego organization," and also perceived "plentiful instances of questionable ego dependability." Despite these warning signals, the psychologist believed that no other treatment except a lengthy analysis provided hope of helping the patient overcome his significant tendencies toward withdrawal, passive aggression, and masochism. Like the interviewer, the psychologist believed that an intensive treatment was not without risk. The division of opinion between the interviewer and the tester regarding whether to recommend psychoanalysis led to a consultation with a senior psychoanalyst, who agreed with the more conservative approach of recommending psychotherapy once or twice a week with a psychoanalyst who might later convert the treatment. Because of the difficulty anticipated with this patient, the consultant recommended referral to an experienced psychotherapist with a lot of patience.

The Psychotherapy Process

Early in psychotherapy, the patient was encouraged to work with his transference reactions, and not infrequently (often defensively) he recalled early childhood experiences relevant to his current feelings. The therapist's interventions were almost entirely interpretive and confrontive, with regard to both the patient's reports of his life situation and to the transference and resistance. At no time was the patient offered support in the form of reassurance, and rarely was adaptive behavior encouraged. The one exception was the therapist's conscious effort to encourage a more benign superego attitude toward dependency feelings, in particular, the patient's penurious lifestyle. The therapist attempted to maintain an attitude of strict neutrality toward the patient's life problems.

Although the patient sought treatment because he believed that his tendency to be too distant and reserved was hampering his professional work, the first phase of therapy revealed a surprising acceptance of these traits. What I had understood as his clear-cut goal began to emerge as a huge question mark: "Is my distance and reserve something that I really want to change?" He obviously enjoyed his lack of involvement and the independence that accompanied his distance, because he viewed this stance as indicative of strength and power. Perhaps others needed relationships with people, but he secretly nurtured the fantasy that he could do without such closeness. This belief was only one side of a deeply felt conflict that he hoped the therapist would counter.

Actually, the patient was reproducing in the therapy his major problem of closeness versus distance, i.e., expressing his open doubts about becoming committed to a working relationship. He intensely feared acknowledging any wish for help. During the first phase of well over a year, his prevailing fantasy was that he was indeed in control of the therapeutic relationship and that his behavior was eliciting certain predicable responses from the therapist. The patient felt compelled to keep his distance because of initial mistrust. The greater his wish for closeness, the greater his fear of abandonment associated with his sudden early loss of both father and mother. From time to time, he spoke of wishing to be in analysis; the neurotic roots of this wish consisted of the fantasy that analysis would be a permanent relationship. In the course of work on this problem of closeness, we touched lightly on the patient's homosexual fears; he felt that giving up his independence would leave him open to sexual assault. As the problem of closeness gradually subsided and the patient became better able to acknowledge his unhappiness with his self-imposed isolation, he was able to recall with some regret that despite critical feelings toward the uncle who had adopted him, he had a fondness for the man, which he could never bring himself to express.

Concomitant with greater closeness in the therapeutic relationship were parallel changes in the patent's interaction with his wife. He also began to engage in increased collaboration with other professionals, partly as a result of becoming more skilled in his work, but also seemingly because of his greater openness with his colleagues and his readiness to undertake joint projects.

In this 12- to 18-month period, the patient was gradually able to give up both his mistrust of the therapist and his stance of pseudoindependence; these would probably have been the opening issues if he had entered analysis from the beginning. This first phase might have been shortened by the greater frequency and intensity of the analytic process, or it might have created heightened anxiety that would have obstructed progress. An important component of this problem, the fear of abandonment when he begins to rely on someone, needed a period of testing and working through before the patient could begin to commit to a relationship. Thus at the beginning of the second year of psychotherapy, the patient was able to give up his view of himself as distant because he wanted to be that way, independent because he was stronger than most, and isolated because he enjoyed it.

The remaining period, or second half, of the psychotherapy dealt largely with the patient's passivity. He characteristically sought male authority figures under whose wings he could feel protected and secure. He tended to eschew an assertive role except as a negativistic reaction to external pressure. He characteristically avoided committing himself to an unequivocal line of action, preferring to keep his options open. He presented himself as someone available to be pursued and courted, finding much gratification when others responded to the bait he dangled. For well over six months he obsessed about the possibility of embarking on further graduate study as a means of achieving greater professional status and financial reward. He incessantly weighed the pros and cons of this decision, suspending many other decisions about his life, until this one was resolved.

One of the major roots of this passivity and obsessionalism was the patient's fear of the oedipal and hostile implications of an assertive role, particularly when it involved competitive wishes toward the therapist. He characteristically avoided overtly hostile thoughts about the therapist. Rather, he tended to become quiet and withdrawn when experiencing such critical feelings, permitting himself only to acknowledge that he was "screening out" negative thoughts. But his professional work gave evidence that he was becoming more active and assertive, and that he did not feel so obligated to find a strong protector against the hazards of self-assertion.

In addition, the patient's masochistic orientation began to soften, as did his frugality and tendency to live a self-depriving existence. For a brief period, he swung almost to the opposite extreme and engaged in several extravagances. He began to exchange his drab garb for more colorful clothes, at times jokingly referring to his identification with the therapist. He noticed a decreasing tendency to become depressed and, even more significant, he claimed that he had less need to "hold onto" his depression.

Although both patient and therapist were gratified with the patient's progress, it was apparent that more could be accomplished. His need to inhibit hostility, his reluctance to commit himself to relationships, his passivity—indeed all the presenting problems—had improved, but further change was considered possible. Moreover, it was dubious whether further progress could be made without a more intensive method such as analysis, so conversion to analysis was jointly decided on during the middle of the third year of psychotherapy.

The question regarding the patient's suitability for analysis had gradually become resolved. After the first three months of analytic treatment, I was impressed by his capacity to work expressively and to use transference interpretations constructively. Throughout my written therapy notes, I made continuing references to the good probability of a positive response to analysis. The major factor delaying the shift was the patient's own characterologically determined inability to decide whether he would continue to reside in the area or leave to pursue further graduate work.

My only doubt concerned his possible need for the stimulation of face-to-face contact. I wondered how much his tendencies toward withdrawal would be exacerbated by the lack of visual contact. At the same time, the patient's gradually increasing positive attachment and his ability to substantially modify his counterdependence diminished my fears that the relationship might revert to a more tenuous one.

Recommending The Shift

The technical problems in converting to analysis depend on when and how the decision to do so is made. If a recommendation for analysis is made at the outset of treatment, and the patient demurs in favor of a less frequent, face-to-face psychotherapy, then the eventual switch to psychoanalysis will be a natural outgrowth of the previous work, inasmuch as the focus of the psychotherapy has helped the patient understand resistances to a more intensive modality.

When the recommendation is not made at the outset and the analyst becomes convinced during the course of treatment that analysis is the preferred modality, the ideal transition occurs when the patient directly or indirectly indicates a wish for a more intensified process. The patient may complain about forgetting important material, such as dreams, because of the long interval between sessions, or may express a wish for more time to work on the emerging material. Under these circumstances, something akin to a mutually agreed-upon decision will result in a transition to analysis without the patient experiencing pressure or manipulation from the therapist.

The most complicated situation, and the one that probably tends to prevail most often, is one in which the recommendation is initiated by the therapist. The therapist's decision is ideally made on the basis of clinical considerations that are in the patient's best interest. But we know that there are usually professional benefits that accrue for analysts who are able to convert a patient to analysis, and however laudable the motive, the analyst's wishes may become a source of technical difficulty. To the extent that analysts have a personal stake in effecting the change of modality, they may overlook the multiple meanings that the recommendation has for the patient.

The patient may, for example, readily accept the analyst's recommendation for changing to analysis, but such acquiescence should be subjected to further exploration. A compliant patient may be inclined to suppress anxieties and doubts, and an overly eager analyst may collude in this. The typical fantasies of a patient following such a recommendation consist of ideas that the therapist is sexually interested in the patient, or that the therapist has newly intensified voyeuristic wishes or wants to exploit the patient for professional advancement. We have observed that this dimension of the pursuer and the pursued, insofar as it is indeed a part of the interaction, not only stimulates a variety of fantasies, but also encourages therapists to overlook such reactions, with inevitable difficulties in the form of heightened resistance and acting out.

This problem is further complicated by the low frequency of sessions during the psychotherapy phase which results in realistic limitation on the time available for fully exploring the patient's reactions to the recommendation for analysis. One must keep in mind that although a more formal analytic procedure is about to begin, it is not the start of the patient's therapeutic experience, but rather an intense part of an ongoing, deepening therapeutic process. Frequently, the therapist will refrain from uncovering and interpreting the fantasies thus stirred on the grounds that such detailed work can be saved for the analytic period. Perhaps some analysts mistakenly believe that a psychotherapy, particularly of low frequency, should not include dealing with the transference. More often than not, failure to deal with the patient's conscious and unconscious reactions will complicate the relationship by precipitating a crisis or leading to a decision to interrupt treatment.

Because my patient had requested analysis from the start, he periodically referred to his disappointment at not receiving it, and some two and one-half years into the psychotherapy, he began to raise the issue more seriously. Basically, he felt pleased with his progress in freeing up his inhibitions and in permitting himself to get closer to others. He correctly perceived that increased progress could best be achieved through psychoanalysis. At the same time, consistent with his characterological stance, he tended to hint and then wait for the therapist to pursue him as a way to feel that the decision to convert rested entirely with him. We explored his fantasies about the change and touched on both the realistic wish to be able to work more intensively and the neurotic wish to have a permanent relationship unthreatened by abandonment. His fantasy about analysis was not simply that it was usually longer than psychotherapy but that it was also eternal and never ending, an understandable wish in light of the traumas of his early life. Even though the switch to psychoanalysis also fit the therapist's professional goals and even though the patient attempted to get the therapist to pursue and pressure him, it was relatively easy to avoid the pitfall of becoming the pursuer insofar as the two of us shared the conviction that any substantial further progress could be attained only through analysis.

Initial Reactions to the Change

What is frequently observed in the initial phase of a converted analysis is a surprisingly marked intensification of affective responses and associational content (Horwitz, 1978; Bernstein, 1983; Levine, 1985). Intense regressive transferences often emerge unexpectedly, revealing accumulated pent-up affects that had not been permitted expression in the previous treatment. A few of the patient behaviors that emerge in the first days and weeks of the change include yearnings for a more primitive symbiotic relationship, fears of this strange "new person" seated out of sight, and tearfulness where none had been present before. The beginning of the analysis, with its more formal trappings, is in fact the middle of an ongoing therapeutic process that is significantly deepening.

This sudden bursting forth of regressive transference reactions, characterized by primitiveness, irrationality, and infantilism, is an important indicator of the difference between psychotherapy and psychoanalysis. The increased frequency of appointments contributes to a lifting of repression and helps prevent important anxiety-laden fantasies from being dissipated by forgetting. A relatively infrequent psychotherapy process tends to engender a quantity of latent transferences that require the setting of analysis for the patient and analyst to fully observe and use the regressive developments that otherwise might remain hidden. The method of free association significantly pressures the patient against withholding and suppression. The unrelenting pressure to "tell all" contributes to a closeness and intensity that usually cannot be achieved in psychotherapy. The lack of visual contact removes the cues that many patients use for reassurance against projected superego disapproval. Not being in eye contact with the analyst also may facilitate the revelation of intimate and embarrassing matters.

An important initial experience is the patient's sense of deprivation associated with no longer being able to see the analyst. Although the deprivation of visual cues has a different meaning for each individual, more often than not the patient experiences a keen feeling of loss insofar as looking at the therapist engenders a sense of presence and support. A counterbalance to this frustration, however, is the heightened sense of timelessness and openendedness in the analytic process, which may stimulate fantasies of unending gratification.

The first month of my patient's analysis elicited many references to the radical change he experienced in making the switch. The change revived feelings of the traumatic separation from his mother at age five. The abrupt separation and his completely new way of life with a relatively unknown uncle and aunt was recapitulated in the sudden changeover. Whereas previously he had emphasized his feelings of relief at being separated from a disturbed mother, he now emphasized his great experience of loss. Although this reaction was partly dictated by the deprivation associated with no longer seeing the psychotherapist face to face, a more significant factor was the experience of going from the familiar to the unfamiliar, from the known to the unknown.

The other side of the coin was the patient's experience of the analysis as a reward and promotion for his successful work in psychotherapy. He had requested analysis in the first place but had been told that it was not recommended because of his "scars of childhood." In a sense, he had proven the experts wrong. But success was a mixed blessing for the patient, particularly insofar as he perceived it as a wished-for but feared triumph over his presumed superiors.

Perhaps the most striking development was this patient's readiness to increase the intensity of his involvement, particularly in relation to the greater frequency of appointments (from two to four hours a week). In contrast to his relatively noncommittal attitude with regard to interruptions of the regular schedule, he responded with surprising intensity to "missing" an analytic hour on the one day of the week he was not schedule to see the analyst. The first week of the analysis, he reported feeling "incomplete" that day. He felt angry when he saw me outside the hour, and wondered if he wanted to see me all the time. "Why is it developing so quickly here when it didn't in therapy?" he asked, referring to the growing bond. It appeared as if a strong cathexis was ready to be attached to something. He was aware of trying to fight off the intensity of the involvement although he also was ready to experience it. This wish for more time was an unexpected development, presumably touched off by the increased frequency of appointments, which meant a promise of limitless nurturance.

Loss of eye contact with the analyst produced feelings of deprivation in the patient the first few weeks, despite the fact that he had often avoided eye contact during psychotherapy. His immediate reaction was a feeling of no longer getting help or guidance. He missed the gratification of immediate feedback based on my facial expression and other nonverbal cues.

Not talking face to face also produced a surge of aggressive feelings toward the analyst which the patient had formerly found difficult to express. He was openly critical that he had not been given analysis in the first place. He experienced interpretations as attacks and criticisms, and he often said forcefully, "To hell with your interpretations; they are not what I want." The quality of the conventional social encounter that exists in face-to-face psychotherapy was no longer present, and the patient seemed freer to speak his mind.

His immediate response to the basic rule was a fear of saying something crazy, accentuated by identification with his psychotic mother. He was afraid that angry feelings would push past his controls, and he became concerned about offending me. He also projected onto me a fear of his mother's impulsiveness, with the idea that perhaps I would blunder or react recklessly or inappropriately.

Finally, the patient's recumbent position on the soft couch led to a number of pleasurable but threatening associations of childhood bliss. He would now be the center of attention, and I would listen to him without interruption. His thoughts turned toward plentiful food, warm beds, soft mattresses, and life on a tropical isle with no demands. This intensification of his dependency needs quickly emerged outside the therapy hours as well, such as wanting more "cuddling" from his wife. He reacted to the cancellation of a regular hour during the first month with intense anger and feelings of deprivation; for the first time during our contact, he reported having left work early to go home and stuff himself with nuts and candy.

The patient's initial reaction to the change was thus a rapid intensification of regressively dependent wishes and formerly avoided aggressive fantasies. The work of the psychotherapy had, of course, contributed to the ease with which these affective reactions occurred. As a result of the previous treatment, the patient was less defensive, more trusting, and more tolerant of his dependency wishes. He did not have to repeat the long process of cautiously surveying the therapeutic terrain before venturing into it. He had developed a potential or latent transference involvement which seemed to burst into full bloom almost from the first moment of reclining on the couch.

Contrary to my expectations, the analysis had produced a more interesting patient. His tendency to long obsessional monologues, embroidered with unnecessary detail and often lacking clearly discernible affect, led me to be concerned that this defensive posture would be enhanced by the analysis. I thought that the patient might become increasingly absorbed in his intellectualizations and fantasies, and that the lack of my visible physical presence might lead to increased distance. Actually, the reverse was true. Greater affective freedom and more intense personal involvement were his almost immediate responses to the analytic situation.

Outcome of Psychoanalysis

The patient continued in the analysis for over 800 hours, a total of five years, and achieved a very satisfactory analytic outcome. A regressive transference neurosis continued to deepen and unfold, and both oedipal and preoedipal conflicts emerged with considerable intensity and were interpreted and worked through mainly via interpretation. Much of the analysis concerned the patient's negative oedipal reaction and its attendant passive and masochistic character problems. He feared having to become a successful adult male lest he be attacked by those he would challenge. He characteristically down-played his accomplishments, professional advancement, and increasing job responsibility, and he attempted to avoid any evidence of competitiveness with the analyst, particularly in professional matters. As we dealt with these oedipal fears, his job performance changed considerably, and he became more direct and outspoken in his dealings with colleagues and a valued member of his professional group. Changes in his marital relationship were slower to occur, in part because of his wife's resistance to accepting his greater assertiveness. On his part, his early fear of provoking his mother into one of her insane rages made it necessary for him to struggle to let himself become less controlled and rational in dealing with his wife. As he began to experience a decreased concern about driving her crazy, he was able to convey the intensity of the frustration that he occasionally experienced with her.

Much of the analysis was conducted with his fantasy that it would be an interminable relationship; the analyst had to actively underline the patient's termination thoughts and help him think seriously about this eventuality. The termination process evoked strong feelings of worthlessness associated with the early losses of both father and mother, based on the idea that neither had considered him important enough to remain with him. His fear of a meaningless and desolate existence without the continuing analytic relationship alternated with his fear of fusing with me and losing his sense of autonomy.

Now, more than ten years after termination, the patient has consolidated the analytic gains in both his professional and marital situations. Despite his earlier reluctance to avoid a leadership role, he has taken on significant job responsibilities, which he carries out successfully. And there is evidence that his family and marital relationships have stabilized and grown in warmth and closeness.

Discussion

Every conversion carries with it a unique combination of common factors as well as specific issues idiosyncratic to that case. We are in an early stage of accumulating knowledge about patients for hom some previous psychotherapy is desirable before commencing psychoanalysis. The two published cases mentioned earlier differed from my patient in some significant ways. Neither was motivated sufficiently for undertaking a major commitment, and the conversion was not made until the patient realized the necessity for a more intensive treatment. In contrast, my patient came seeking analysis, but the diagnostic team that performed the initial workup reached a consensus that questioned his analyzability and instead recommended starting psychotherapy with an analyst who might later convert the treatment to psychoanalysis.

Despite their differing recommendations regarding the preferred mode of treatment, both the interviewer and the tester agreed that the patient's ego intactness was sufficiently in doubt as to make him less than an ideal candidate for psychoanalysis. They both saw evidence of primary process intrusions, vulnerability of reality testing, and a potential for further decompensation under stress. On the other hand, neither of them saw clear signs of underlying disorganization.

When I received the examination reports in conjunction with this referral, I concurred with the conservative position of the interviewer. To some extent, I was influenced by my work with the Menninger Foundation Psychotherapy Research Project, in which several patients with questionable indications for psychoanalysis had been underdiagnosed and emerged from analysis with unfavorable results (Horwitz, 1974). At the same time, I viewed the psychotherapy as a "trial for analysis" and kept in mind the possibility of conversion. My psychotherapy progress notes clearly indicate this line of thinking and, moreover, point to a slowly increasing conviction that this patient was indeed analyzable. At the end of the first six months, I noted: "I have been surprised with the patient's capacity to respond with lively interest and appropriate affect when the therapist points out transference reactions. I am struck by his flexibility and ego resources, considering his highly traumatic early life." Then some 15 months after the start of psychotherapy, I was impressed with his slow but growing attachment to me and his identification with his warm, interested uncle who had adopted him at age five.

My notes at that time clearly reflected my belief that the patient was analyzable, although the issue did not come up until several months later, and the conversion was not made until still a few months after that. The delay was compounded by many factors, including the patient's long period of uncertainty about whether to leave Topeka to pursue further studies. In addition, although the patient began hinting about his interest in reconsidering analysis about two years into the psychotherapy, he characteristically required me to become the pursuer to reassure him of my interest. The only question regarding conversion that I included in my records was whether the loss of visual contact with the patient would somehow weaken the attachment and foster the patient's tendencies to emotional distance and withdrawal. Instead, the reverse occurred insofar as the patient's closeness and bonding with the therapist became more manifest shortly after starting the analysis.

In this case, a trial period of psychotherapy was undoubtedly indicated for further diagnostic clarification. We should also consider, however, the extent to which this case may have fallen into the category of patients who needed psychotherapy for ego strengthening before undergoing a more intense and stressful procedure. Although a few writers have referred to the desirability of such a sequence (Stone, 1961; Blanck and Blanck, 1974), there is no substantial case material to clearly illustrate the structural changes in the patient that made analysis possible. In discussing the present patient we must, of necessity, engage in speculation and some questions will necessarily remain unanswered. Was the conservative procedure of a preceding psychotherapy necessary, or could the patient have begun analysis immediately? Would the slowly developed therapeutic alliance that occurred in psychotherapy have been speeded up or slowed down if the patient had started immediately in psychoanalysis? Further, would he have experienced an iatrogenic regression without a preparatory psychotherapy?

In considering these issues, let us examine separately two of the major difficulties that the patient experienced in the first year of psychotherapy: First, his great fear and reluctance to let down his barriers against getting attached, becoming dependent, and permitting himself to begin working in treatment. Initially, he presented himself in a year-long first phase of treatment as being uncertain about whether he wanted to change his rigidly defended distance. His character armor produced uncomfortable reactions of aloneness and isolation, but it also gave him the satisfaction of being able to manage on his own, free of worry about the whims of others and imbued with a sense of strength about his independence. On the other hand, he was consciously seeking treatment to change this pattern and, at the very least, he was concerned about its effect on his professional work. His need for emotional distance was partly related to fear that close relationships inevitably lead to painfully sudden abandonments. Evidence that progress had been made in this sphere occurred only when the patient was able to indicate clearly that he did indeed want to overcome his distance-taking defense, in relation to both the therapist and others.

The patient obviously needed time to develop a sense of trust in the reliability of the therapist, specifically that he would not be abandoned suddenly and without warning. This issue, which was interpreted consistently throughout the first year of psychotherapy, might have become attenuated sooner with the greater frequency of psychoanalysis. But the patient also needed time to experience the consistency and reliability of the therapist. And from this point of view, the frequency of sessions would probably not have had a significant impact, either positive or negative.

The second major presenting paradigm, related to the first, was the patient's fear of fusion, loss of autonomy, and need to avoid the feeling of being smothered by too much closeness. This underlying fear made it necessary for him to prove to himself that in any close relationship he could retain the reins of control. This dynamic underlay his passive-aggressivity and stubbornness, as well as his smugly superior attitude toward attempts to get him to change. One of his wife's chief complaints was that he constantly encouraged her to develop other interests and other relationships because he found it difficult to tolerate her strong attachment to and need for him. In the early phases of psychotherapy, he took pleasure in the fantasy that the content he presented required me to engage in certain predictable interventions, thus reassuring himself that he was indeed in control. His early experiences with his mother, whose own ego boundaries were clearly deficient and who relied on her young son to bolster her failing reality testing, undoubtedly contributed greaterly to his need to ward off possible intrusions from others.

Is previous psychotherapy necessary to deal with this primitive struggle regarding ego boundaries? I propose that patients with such an intense struggle fare better in the early phases of treatment with face-to-face psychotherapy. The visual contact with the therapist, as well as the more equal feeling created by sitting up, gives the patient a greater sense of control. Also, since psychotherapy involves more interactive dialogue, this patient may have had less difficulty in experiencing the fantasy of being in control of my interventions. Patients in analysis have fewer cues regarding the reality of the analyst's person and behavior and hence may have a more difficult time in overcoming boundary and fusion problems sufficiently to enable them to work productively in the analysis.

Thus, with regard to the patient's initial mistrust of the therapist based mainly on his fear of sudden abandonment, there was probably a necessary period required for developing a sense of trust and a similar length of time was most likely needed in either psychotherapy or analysis. On the other hand, the patient's basic "need/fear" dilemma, his wish for symbiosis, and his fear of fusion may indeed have been resolved more effectively, i.e., with the requisite degree of gradualness, in the less intense face-to-face process that allows the patient to feel a greater sense of control.

Acknowledgment

I am grateful to Dr. Ernst A. Ticho for his encouragement and guidance in my undertaking this work.

REFERENCES

Bernstein, S. B. (1983). Treatment preparatory to psychoanalysis. *J. Amer. Psychoanal. Assn.,* 31:363–390.

Blanck, G. & Blanck, R. (1974). *Ego psychology: Theory and Practice.* New York: Columbia Univ. Press.

Eissler, K. R. (1953). The effect of the structure of the ego on psychoanalytic technique. *J. Amer. Psychoanal. Assn.,* 1:104–143.

Freud, S. (1913). On the beginning of treatment (further recommendations on the technique of psycho-anlysis I.) *S.E.,* 12.

Gill, M. M. (1954). Psychoanalysis and exploratory psychotherapy. *J. Amer. Psychoanal. Assn.,* 2:771–797.

Gill, M. M. (1988). Converting psychotherapy into psychoanalysis. *Contemp. Psychoanal.,* 24:262–274.

Horwitz, L. (1974). *Clinical Prediction in Psychotherapy.* New York: Jason Aronson.

_____ (1978). A comparison of psychoanalysis and psychotherapy with the same patient. Unpublished.

Kernberg, O. F. (1982). To teach or not to teach psychotherapy techniques in psychoanalytic education. In *Psychotherapy: Impact on Psychoanalytic Training,* ed. E. Joseph & R. S. Wallerstein. New York: Int. Univ. Press.

Levine, H. B. (1985). Psychotherapy as the initial phase of psychoanalysis. *Int. Rev. Psychoanal.,* 12:285–297.

Panel (1987). Conversion of Psychotherapy to Psychoanalysis, C. P. Fisher, Reporter. *J. Amer. Psychoanal. Assn.,* 35:713–726.

Shapiro, D. (1980). Report of the Ad Hoc Committee on Psychoanalytic Practice, American Psychological Association. Unpublished.

Stone, L. (1961). *The Psychoanalytic Situation.* New York: Int. Univ. Press.

Menninger Clinic
Box 829
Topeka, KS 66601

A Developmental View of Converting Psychotherapy to Psychoanalysis

NATHAN SCHLESSINGER, M.D.

THE CONVERSION FROM PSYCHOTHERAPY to psychoanalysis is a topic of formidable dimensions, engaging as it does, the perennial issue of defining the two modes of treatment in terms of theory and technique. Shifting definitions of psychoanalysis both as process and treatment have contributed to the complexity of the discussion.

In a survey on psychoanalytic practice, Shapiro et al. (1981) reported that one eighth of the analytic cases had previous psychotherapy. The numbers of psychotherapists have been increasing at an accelerating rate in the interim, and clinic experience at intake demonstrates an accompanying rise in frequency of previous psychotherapy among prospective analysands. Practically speaking, the "pure, uncontaminated" analytic case is apt to become an endangered species. Furthermore, there is a growing opinion (Panel, 1987) that some cases give positive indications for previous psychotherapy. The question, then, is, what theoretical and technical considerations determine an appropriate conversion.

In this paper, I consider the topic of conversion from psychotherapy to psychoanalysis in the broadest context, whether the conversion is conducted by the same analyst or after referral to another analyst. I offer two case examples from my own clinical

Dr. Schlessinger is Associate Dean for Clinical Services, Institute for Psychoanalysis, Chicago; Clinical Professor of Psychiatry, College of Medicine, University of Illinois.

experience as a basis for discussion. As an introduction, a historical review of the essential issues involved in conceptualizing conversions seems appropriate.

Psychoanalysis, in its origins, was most concerned with divesting itself of suggestion and hypnosis, the prevailing techniques of psychotherapy (Gill, 1954). Freud's major focus was on a rational analysis of symptoms that uncovered their unconscious ramifications. Since that interpretive endeavor had to be protected from any hint of suggestion, psychotherapy was regarded as an alien and objectionable method. With Freud's conceptualizations and revisions of analytic theory and technique in subsequent decades, the analytic enterprise mobilized renewed interest in its relationship to psychotherapy.

In the major panel discussions centering on psychotherapy and psychoanalysis in the fifties (Panel, 1953a, 1953b, 1954), the distinction between analysis and psychotherapy no longer hinged on suggestion alone. Psychotherapy was applied psychoanalysis. Bandler (Panel, 1953a) suggested that psychoanalysis provided a rational, predictable, and communicable frame of reference for treatment. He described psychotherapy as the exploration of a (psychological) terrain, mapped out by using psychoanalytic concepts as a compass. Rangell (Panel, 1954) defined analysis as the development of a transference neurosis and its resolution by interpretation alone. He drew a sharp distinction between the development and resolution of a transference neurosis and an interactive approach with intermediate forms of stability that did not come to such an end point. Bibring (Panel, 1954) outlined the essential ingredients of psychotherapy as suggestion, abreaction, clarification, interpretation, and manipulation. He noted that while all these technical and curative agents might be utilized in an analytic process and in psychotherapy, the curative principle in analysis was the primacy of insight through interpretation. Gill (1954) believed that analysis addressed character and the unconscious whereas psychotherapy focused on symptoms and remedial actions.

The definitions of analysis in these debates showed some

consensus regarding an oedipal paradigm. In effect, earlier developmental problems were the domain of psychotherapy. However, budding theoretical controversy in the debates of the fifties centered on pregenital and interpersonal clinical phenomena in the analytic process. Fromm-Reichmann (Panel, 1954) noted some controversy about libido theory versus interpersonal concepts, suggesting that ego psychology with its focus on the management of anxiety brought into conjunction an approach to sexual conflicts and the desire for closeness. Waelder (Panel, 1953b) emphasized the return of the repressed to explain neurosis in an intrapsychic context and distinguished it from interpersonal adaptation, which might require such techniques as Alexander's (Panel, 1954) corrective emotional experience. Greenacre (Panel, 1954) believed pregenital features were important in every case, and considered them phenomena that must be analyzed and not simply interpreted as regression.

In the 1979 Panel, Wallerstein noted that, in the two decades that had elasped since the fifties, psychoanalytic theory again had grown in complexity, influenced by psychoanalytic developmental theory, object relations theory, and self psychology, and encompassing the contributions of Mahler, Jacobson, Kernberg, and Kohut, among others. With Zetzel (1965) and Greenson (1967) elaborating on the concept of the analytic alliances, the scope of psychoanalysis had widened. While therapy once again could be defined as applied psychoanalysis, what distinguished analysis from therapy was less sharply delineated, as earlier developmental states entered the analytic situation.

Dewald (Panel, 1979) defined psychotherapy as changes at a derivative level in selected conflicts with a limited depth of regression aimed at symptom relief, behavioral change, or reestablishment of psychic equilibrium. In his view, the patient made conscious and unconscious use of therapeutic interventions, to provide psychological reinforcement and transference gratification. Interactional responses provided more of a stimulus for internalization and identification with the therapist. In patients with developmental arrest or ego defects, the therapist's role as provider of a holding environment was more significantly engaged. Kernberg, the other participant of that Panel (1979) said that in severe psychopathology, treatment centered on the systematic interpretation of defenses to improve ego functions and to permit the transformation of primitive transferences. There was a need to define the interaction of self and object components and affects and to integrate them, since they were dissociated and split off. Michels (Panel, 1979) thought that psychoanalysis could be differentiated more by process than by technique in that it was characterized by a relatively spontaneous evolution. In his metaphor, the psychoanalyst was a naturalist, the therapist as engineer.

In the panel on conversion of psychotherapy to psychoanalysis (Panel, 1987), with Gill, Horwitz, Kernberg, and E. Ticho as participants, consensus about such a procedure was favorable, even as conducted by the same analyst, reversing a long-standing prejudice against that procedure. Some new elements emerged in the ongoing debate. There was the recognition of one kind of exploratory, expressive psychotherapy conducted in a nondirective manner by a neutral therapist in which transferences were resolved by interpretation, a category earlier mentioned by Oremland (Panel, 1987). These interpretations were regarded as incomplete rather than inexact. Such a therapy could be readily converted to a full-scale analysis, a view shared by Ticho. Horwitz (Panel, 1987) noted that in cases with serious resistances and dubious indications for analysis or even apparent contraindications to analysis, an exploratory expressive psychotherapy might resolve the situation in favor of analysis. He cited Bernstein (1983) as describing the successful use of a preparatory therapy to cope with a patient's intense fears of regression.

Levine (1985) described a case in which psychotherapy was the initial phase of a successful thoroughgoing analysis. He observed that previous psychotherapy may help to clarify and analyze the fears of entering analysis; it may also help to develop the necessary reservoir of trust and the capacity for curiosity, self-observation, and openness for an analytic process. The preliminary psychotherapy, in his view, provides a gradual and controlled path to analytic regression and offers preparation to forestall potentially disruptive acting out by interpretive interventions.

The 1987 Panel recognized that psychotherapy may be useful as a preparation for analysis with varying provisos. Ticho thought that clear distinctions between therapy and analysis should be maintained. Kernberg argued for the use of the most analytic mode of treatment that seemed at all feasible at the time of diagnosis and said that conversion should take place in the first year of treatment. Gill, presenting the most extreme view, defined analysis as essentially a focus on transference without special regard for frequency of sessions or the use of the couch. As he pointed out, with such a definition, the conversion to analysis would rarely arise for the analyst practicing his discipline.

A Current View of Psychotherapy and Psychoanalysis

Wallerstein (1983) observed that the analytic debate of the fifties regarding the attempt to differentiate psychotherapy from psychoanalysis could be restated in 1969 and again in 1983 with little resolution and few answers to the questions he posed in Rome in 1969. His conclusion was essentially that the distinctions between various forms of treatment would be best served by a strategic retreat to the classical definition of analysis as a method of treatment suitable for the interpretation of psychoneurotic conflicts. Such a treatment centered on the oedipal phase of development and its resolution. Analyzable patients were presumed to have had a relatively benign early development with unimpaired capacities to engage in an analytic effort in which interpretation alone would constitute the therapeutic modality. It would be logical enough then to categorize patients with earlier developmental problems as suitable for psychotherapy.

Advances in analytic theory and technique over the past two decades have resulted from an exploration of derivatives of early childhood development as they enter the analytic process. A current view of the two modes of treatment depends precisely on an effort to integrate these advances. My research and clinical experience have led me to a developmental view quite at odds with Wallerstein's suggestion.

Follow-up studies I have conducted, in collaboration with Fred Robbins, through the Clinic of the Institute for Psychoanalysis in Chicago over the past 25 years revealed the unfavorable consequences of the application of an oedipal paradigm with inadequate attention to earlier developmental derivatives in a variety of neurotic syndromes and character disorders. The persistent clinical issues were states of overstimulation, frantic efforts at solution, pseudomastery, and attitudes of compliance. As character defenses and patterns of response with roots in dyadic experiences, they limited the effectiveness of interpretive efforts directed at structural conflicts. In our view, such phenomena indicated defects and distortions in structure that coexisted with psychoneurotic symptoms.

We concluded that the regularity and frequency of sessions and the analyst's sensitive attention and tactful interventions provided a psychotherapeutic effect, helpful in the short run, but obscuring pathological early developmental derivatives in the analytic process, which became more evident only with termination. In two of the cases reported in our monograph (Schlessinger & Robbins, 1983), further analytic efforts that did address these early derivatives interpretively in a transference context resulted in significant improvement, confirming the value of an approach to the patient based on a developmental point of view. In corroboration on Greenacre's (Panel, 1954) comment, our studies have emphasized the need to view such psychopathology not simply as a regressive defense against oedipal material but as a significant focus of analytic interest and, moreover, a critical determinant in the outcome of the process.

What then constitutes the essential distinction between psychotherapy and psychoanalysis? To create polar positions for psychotherapy as supportive and psychoanalysis as not clearly begs the question. The two modes of treatment share a common ground over the whole range of psychotherapy and employ a wide variety of interventions from supportive to interpretive in their treatment.

One difference is in the nature of the goals. In psychotherapy, the goals are more limited, directed at relief of symptoms, amelioration of problems, the understanding of sectors of pathological function and their reparative solutions. Psychoanalysis is a method of treatment for characterological problems and their accompanying neurotic symptomatology that involves an effort at total personality reorganization across the course of development.

More specifically, in the management of early developmental derivatives, the purpose in an analysis is to create conditions that enable the analyst to engage these derivatives in a transference context and to identify and explore their developmental significance; in psychotherapy, interventions are more apt to be made for their effect in influencing or counteracting disturbing affects and obstacles to the limited goals of treatment.

I suggest an additional major distinction between therapy and analysis in instances where psychotherapy is conducted predominantly in an interpretative mode with regard to conflict, behavior, and transferences. I would call psychotherapy applied analysis in the sense that it utilizes the acquired knowledge and techniques of analysis for the specific purpose of achieving whatever goals have been set for the therapy. Psychoanalysis, in contrast, is a collaborative effort at a process of discovery.

Finally, with regard to enduring change in the two modes of treatment, the nature of internalizations is a crucial distinction. One may variously consider transmuting internalizations in the acquisition of functions; the internalization of a benign, calming, pacifying and encouraging object representation; and the internalization of a self-analytic function in coping with conflict. The Menninger Study (Kernberg et al., 1972) concluded that enduring structural changes may be brought about by supportive measures alone; in effect, a positive identification with the therapist. In our monograph, we have described such a result in analysis as a therapeutic patch on early developmental problems, vulnerable to further vicissitudes of life and requiring further analysis. In psychoanalysis, the goal is identifications with the functions of the analyst rather than his person, following an analysis of the transference in infantile precursors and developmental distortions.

The Process of Conversion

The conceptualization and management of a first phase of analysis is critical when converting from psychotherapy to analysis. This phase constitutes an induction into the analytic process. Whether the conversion is by the same analyst or otherwise, previous psychotherapy offers significant guideposts to problems in induction of an analytic process if the analyst is attentive to what has characterized the alliance and the process in the psychotherapy—the degree to which it repeated or departed from, utilized or engaged past relationships in addressing tension regulation and the management of conflict. The first phase of analysis sees movement from a therapeutic alliance to an analytic alliance, setting the stage for a collaborative effort at discovery in the unfolding transference neurosis. Establishing an analytic alliance requires careful attention to the engagement of neurotic conflicts, deficits, and distortions as they are reflected in defensive character patterns and problems in communication and in the capacity for perception and processing of experiences.

Two cases may serve to illustrate the process of conversion and provide a clinical ground for a further elaboration of the issues involved.

Case 1

The first case I converted directly from a preliminary psychotherapy, after several months of treatment, twice a week. The patient was a 28-year-old graduate student in history who entered treatment because of problems in completing her dissertation. On the surface she displayed consummate skills as a collaborator. She was friendly, bright, and eager to receive the suggestions and advice of her adviser. She could discuss the intellectual ramifications of his ideas and bring supporting evidence to bear on them, in his presence. She sought and gained his approval thereby as an immediate and pressing motive for her participation. In the privacy of her study as she attempted to review her conversions with her adviser, her creativity and productivity were sharply compromised. She felt painfully blocked in writing her thesis and became convinced of her need for treatment.

Her early childhood was marked by the death of her father when she was three years old. Her mother, an artistic, dependent woman, remarried when the patient was five, after an interlude in which she and her mother lived with her grandparents. Her stepfather was a successful businessman, benevolent, albeit authoritarian and self-righteous. The newly reconstituted family restored a sense of security to the child who had responded to the death of her father with a change of character from an inquisitive, active youngster with an engaging manner to an intimidated and fearful girl.

She experienced some phobic symptoms, and her life became rule-bound and controlled. Her experiences were dominated by parental expectations and parental guidance. She developed a remarkable capacity to read cues and respond to the needs and views of people around her. Her own early history was obscured by the family's effort to lay to rest any memories connected with her biological father. A spark of her old vivacity and interest persisted, so that she learned to express contrary opinions cloaked in humor, with a ready retreat to compliance if she went too far. Her course through life was monitored by her family through her college career close to home and an early marriage to an older man who met the family requirements.

She had returned to graduate school to contend with a prevailing sense of boredom. The focus of her interest in her dissertation in the field of early American history reflected a frustrated curiosity about her own origins. It created a conflicted motivation, a mixture of compliant inhibition and the determination to find a way to gratify her desire to know.

Her defensive collaborative style with her adviser concealed her conflicted motives and disturbing affects in an uneasy compromise. She was imaginative and creative at times with her subject, secretly, transiently, at a distance, but her capacity to remain in touch with her personal reactions to the material crumbled as she attempted to put it to use. The psychotherapeutic collaboration mirrored her experience with her adviser. She rapidly established a friendly relationship with the therapist, with an idealizing transference, supported by an intent regard for any cues in verbal and nonverbal behavior that would create safe conditions for her experience. She responded warmly to the sessions, enjoyed the opportunity to describe her experiences to an attentive listener, and avidly accepted any interventions. Her anxieties were superficially relieved in a nonspecific manner by the relationship itself. She was able to pursue intellectually any suggestion or question directed to her experiences and to enjoy the intellectual exchange, but in the service of enhancing her acceptability. She regarded her dreams as strange, alien, and without meaningful connection to her life. They were essentially fragmentary, if she recalled them at all. What she did recall often expressed a suspicion and mistrust quite at odds with her conscious perceptions and was affectively unavailable.

It rapidly became evident that the compliant collaboration with her adviser and her therapist was obligatory, since she needed and used it for permission to pursue her research and scholarship at all, however compromised the effort. Her problems in self-observation and self-assertion were somewhat concealed by her deft use of cues and intellectual competence. Any disagreement or question caused her great difficulty. In her experience, conflict was deicded by authoritative opinion. In the therapy, if the cues she sought to divine my attitude and opinion were insufficient to give her a sense of direction, she asked questions about what patients usually felt or thought under such and such circumstances, as a statistical approach to defining herself. As she came to feel secure in the therapeutic relationship we had established, she accepted with some relief my efforts to focus on the nature of the collaboration and the anxieties it was intended to contain. She enjoyed a kind of humorous acknowledgment and a gradual capacity for self-perception of the quandaries this mode of behavior created for her generally with friends, relatives, and colleagues and specifically with her adviser and her therapist.

When I recommended an analysis, after we had identified the problems she faced in a convincing and ego-syntonic fashion in the course of several months of treatment, she approached it cautiously as a prospect and then decided to proceed. The use of the couch sharply decreased available cues and was therefore a source of distress to her, as was the loss of eye contact. These reactions became readily evident when the patient had to sit up once or twice in an hour and turn to look at me, an activity that was smoothly executed as though it were for the purpose of adding emphasis to something being communicated. Her concern about the analyst's response and her need for cues were interpreted and related to fearfulness about whether she could express what she thought and felt without a loss of attention or outright disapproval. The threat of disagreements with her parents and particularly any angry reactions at them became a significant focus of the analytic work. Suppressed anger was a frequent ingredient in her interactions with her parents since they maintained a conviction that they knew exactly what was right for her. Any assertion of her own views or wishes in conflict with her parents would be dismissed or sharply contested. Her reliance on statistics and facts had been mobilized as a response to such interactions.

For the most part she had learned to comply, but the impulse to express outrageous contradictions remained with her. Her rebelliousness persisted as a saving grace, shielded by her sense of humor. She was able to be outspoken and even had a reputation for it with her friends, with the idea that of course it did not correspond to what she really thought. She was surprised at how pervasively the constraints resulting from parental guidance invested every aspect of her life. A secret source of her compliance that slowly came into focus was the buried reaction to her father's death, with some magical notions about her role in it and responsibility for it. Talking about her father was itself treading on forbidden ground, and she met the opportunity with surprise and tears. In spite of (and because of) her parents' valiant efforts to protect her from her feelings about his death, she realized that she harbored feelings about being an orphan, a confusion about family connections, and a deep sense of loss.

As a concomitant to the characteristic mode of relating to the analyst and reporting and processing information, her experience with her dissertation offered convincing corroboration of the nature of the problem and the potential for a solution. Her work went slowly with a heavy reliance on her meetings with her adviser, bending her views to his expressed opinions, thereby warping her scholarship and intensifying her conflicted motivations. The problem became more acute when her adviser had to take a three-month leave. She sought a replacement for guidance. There were a new set of opinions and cues, and her anxiety mounted. By this time her problems in self-expression had been sufficiently engaged and analyzed that we could readily shed light on her experience with the dissertation. The realization that the threat of separation and loss was a very significant factor in maintaining her compliance had a profound effect on her, coming as it did in conjunction with her dawning awareness about her reactions to her father's death.

Reactions to weekend interruptions and a brief vacation from her analysis further intensified her conscious grasp of how she responded to the threat of separation. She took courage from the fund of insight she was acquiring and the ongoing changes initiated in her analysis. Her dreams had become less fragmentary and more revealing as she recognized her anger and oppositional trends and her accompanying fear and suspicion. With her adviser, she began to use her own ideas generated by a closer study of her available records. She began to consider her adviser's impressions and reactions as an interesting addition to her own ideas and to question differences in approach with regard to what the contradictions might reveal. As she was able to risk advancing her own reading of the texts, a gradual and very constructive change was introduced in the nature of her collaboration. To her surprise, her added enthusiasm and self-expression yielded a positive response from her adviser and an easing of the tensions that had come to characterize their meetings.

The preparatory psychotherapy in this case was essentially exploratory. It permitted the development of an idealizing transference as a necessary supportive measure for this phobic woman. Her need for cues in a face-to-face interaction could be gratified as she reenacted the collaboration she had established with her adviser. When she could tolerate the identification of the nature of the collaboration as a problem, with an accompanying focus on the anxieties it concealed, accept it with some humor, and evidence some curiosity about its origins, it was possible to recommend analysis.

The analytic work in this first phase of her analysis addressed her problems in a dyadic framework. Her collaborative style repeated the relationship she had established with her mother. Her need for approval was a paramount issue for her as a child after the death of her father. Any separation was a threat. Her own thoughts and fantasies were off limits. Communication was for the purpose of seeking rules to guide her at every step and permission for acceptable thoughts and feelings. Her ability to think about what she learned and processed was sharply circumscribed, interfering with any creative endeavor. In character, communication, and processing of information, she identified with her mother and acceded to her wishes, a process that had begun earlier but was intensified by her father's death. The reactions to her father's death had to remain a secret, initiating a phobic response to her thoughts and fantasies.

For this patient, with her great need to comply and please, any authoritative approach to her problems would have been accepted with alacrity and remained as meaningless substantively as the exchanges with her adviser. The development of a capacity for a meaningful collaboration constituted an induction into the analytic process with the prospect of a genuine research into the further vicissitudes of her own early history and her dissertation topic.

Case 2

The patient was a mental health professional in his late thirties who complained of an inability to develop an enduring relationship with a woman and recurrent episodes of anxiety accompanied by withdrawal at work. His father was a successful engineer who conveyed the impression that all was perfect and under his control. His mother was an ailing, masochistic woman completely dominated by her husband and often incapacitated by her symptoms. She accepted a depreciated role, in which her illnesses included a concealed expression of her discontent, but she was devoted to her husband without conscious question or contradiction.

The essential response of the patient to this family configuration was an overidealization of his father accompanied by an exaggerated compliance. Experiences of working with his father included his serving him and applauding his wisdom. He grew up with a depreciated view of himself and an obedient attention to chores and paternal expectations. His efforts did not earn him any special regard; they were taken for granted. His family paid no particular attention to his plans or career choice. He chose a college that would not prove a burden financially to his father. When he left home, he felt as though he ceased to exist for his family. An estrangement from his father ensued, with a marked disinclination to please him by means of customary adulation. He had a tendency to act out in self-destructive ways in brief liaisons with depreciated women and some exaggerated preoccupation with bodily ills. His increasing distress prompted him to enter psychotherapy.

A prolonged insight-oriented treatment over several years had resulted in some improvement in his self-esteem and a cessation of his self-destructive acting out. Although the therapy was conducted in an interpretive mode, the improvement rested on a reconstitution of the idealized relationship with his father. The therapist's interventions and interpretations were invariably accepted. The decision to terminate was made after the patient seemed to have formed a promising relationship with a woman of some professional attainments. The improvements did not persist. In his work, he displayed an arrogance in behavior and lack of attention to his colleagues that created inevitable conflicts. His relationship with his girlfriend was terminated by her, to his surprise. He had attempted to adapt to her demands as her interest flagged and to engage in a kind of programmed behavior calculated to maintain her good will. He made no effort to confront what really was at issue between them nor could he discern it. When he determined to seek analysis after consulting his therapist, he was unable to explain what had happened to disrupt the relationship.

In the diagnostic assessment of the analysis, the ambiguities and incomplete grasp of circumstances in the patient's communications were striking. His account of the treatment did reveal his idealization of the therapist. He had little conviction about anything he had learned in his treatment, although he could repeat some of the insights he had gained. The interpretations and reconstructions he had arrived at were essentially pseudosolutions with little meaning beyond pleasing his therapist. I concluded that compliance had robbed his therapeutic experience of genuine meaning, and I conveyed this impression to the patient. The patient accepted my formulation with the same alacrity he had his therapist's views.

As the first phase of the analysis unfolded, the problem was engaged. The patient's expectation of authoritative explanations about his experiences and dreams was frustrated. It developed that ambiguities and fragmentary accounts of experiences had been rounded out and filled in by his previous therapist, apparently on the grounds that any hints had to be utilized because of the intensity of the repression. Instead, the avoidance of significant thought and affect proceeded out of compliance and passive submission to an all-knowing father in an effort to identify with his strength and wisdom as a planned approach to life. His behavior corresponded remarkably with the self-effacing conduct of his mother.

The idea that his analyst was truly hearing him he found astonishing and disconcerting. His programmed approach to relationships had the quality of a pseudoidentity. Reality processing was somewhat embarrassed because the impact of events did not readily penetrate the programmed shield. His native intelligence and talent permitted a sufficient approximation to realistic function to obscure the nature of the problem in ordinary circumstances. In understudying his father, he could be arrogant, determined, and efficient. He occasionally had a partial recognition of his identification with his mother with a reaction of abhorrence because of her depreciated role and the accompanying threat of homosexuality. The deeper roots of his identification with his mother were brought into focus as a significant part of the analytic process.

The engagement of the character defense and its accompanying mode of communication and coping in the opening phase of the analysis, as it was repeated in the transference, created the basis for developing an analytic alliance. With the occurrence of any conflict in relation to family, colleagues, and friends, involving competitiveness, ambition, or sexual concerns, the tendency to engage his character defense was promptly in evidence. He turned to ambiguous accounts and the role of passive recipient of the analyst's knowledge, and the use of a programmed approach came back into view. Any departure from his mother's solution aroused the fear of loss of his mother and the recognition of his rage at her. His character defense, his mode of communication, and his method of processing information were a recurring focus of analytic work with a deepening understanding of their origins and the development of an analytic alliance that permitted a genuinely inquisitive and realistic engagement with inner conflict in relation to the outside world.

Discussion

My central thesis with regard to the conversion of psychotherapy to analysis is that it requires attention to the whole range of the patient's development. Specifically the analyst must address defensive patterns in the patient stemming from early interactions in a dyadic frame of reference that present as character defenses, problems in communication, in perception, and in the processing of information. The effort to engage these defenses and distortions in ego functions in the first phase of an analysis seems crucial if the patient is to participate as a genuine collaborator in setting up an analytic alliance. Such an effort is especially important in the conversion from a psychotherapy, which has often facilitated transference repetitions in the therapeutic alliance and utilized them for a limited purpose within the treatment setting. Character defenses and distortions in ego functions are inevitably part of the ongoing analysis of intrapsychic conflict as well, with the goal of developing an autonomous self-analytic function as an outcome of the analysis.

A careful diagnostic appraisal facilitates the conversion to analysis by identifying problems in the mode of collaboration in the psychotherapy. The presenting defensive patterns of behavior with their dyadic roots are persistent, repetitive, and adaptive as a means of establishing relationships. They reveal their alloplastic quality in that they readily elicit responses that correspond to the patient's expectations. They are accessible and available for identification in the presenting facade of the patient and the initial interactions with the analyst.

The collaborative effort in the previous psychotherapy serves as a rich source of information for diagnostic purposes. The nature of the relationship established in psychotherapy has been described as more interactive by a number of analysts, with more manifest and continuous feedback in a face-to-face situation. In such an interactional context, the therapist may more readily permit transference gratifications and identifications free play in the effort to achieve specific limited goals. The therapist's countertransference reaction may be to identify with the patient's style and to respond with a complementary, facilitating role. When the previous therapy has been characterized by such a repetition in the transference and countertransference, the interaction provides a kind of sanction for the patient's expectations in the opening phase of the analysis and it requires particular tact and clarification to establish an analytic alliance.

The diagnostic appraisal must also address the question of analyzability. It is clearly not the case that all patients are analyzable, because all patients have a variety of developmental problems. The regression induced by an analytic process for the purpose of understanding the origin of maladaptive patterns of behavior in their infantile and childhood context creates stress. The use of the couch with its loss of eye contact and all the cues that enter into the usual adult reality-oriented communication is a challenge to the patient's capacity for object constancy and for dyadic reality processing. Free association, as a basic rule, directs the patient to set aside all the rules of conduct that ordinarily restrict the extent and depth of the communicative interaction.

Attention to fantasies and dreams, to childhood memories, and to associations on the periphery of conscious experience challenge the patient's capacity for processing his experience beyond the conventional mode. The patient's desire for relief from suffering arouses the deepest longings for magical interventions. The analytic process is predicted on the assumption that the patient has the resources at the outset to begin to participate in the creation of a therapeutic play within the play of everyday life and to find within it the strength and insight for better solutions to his problems. The effort is inevitably collaborative, and the demand on the patient is not to be taken lightly. Attention to the fate of early developmental derivatives in the interactions of the previous therapy raises questions and sheds light on these issues as they are brought to a critical test in the first phase of the analysis.

With regard to character defenses, in my first example, the therapy itself was directed to identifying the problems about collaborative efforts and engaging the patient's interest and curiosity about their origins. The patient's self-effacing style and excessive reliance on advisers reflected a phobic avoidance initiated in her earliest experiences with separation-individuation. In my second example, the relationship between patient and therapist repeated the past, establishing an idealizing transference and a major defense of compliance as the prevailing mode for the entire treatment.

Communication problems in psychotherapy as in analysis may enter the process silently, as a seemingly successful adaptation. The first patient's overriding motivation in communication was to gain approval and permission for her thoughts and activities. She experienced independent thought and fantasy as dangerous, threatening separation and loss. Her attention to nonverbal and verbal cues was highly developed as a means of guiding her own communication. Free association, including the reporting of dreams and fantasies, was a considerable challenge to this patient's resources. The problem had been identified in therapy with some amelioration in response to a friendly, supportive, clarifying attitude. In the conversion to analysis, it was engaged in the transference, with an elaboration of its origins in the relationship with her mother and its intensification after her father's death.

The second patient's use of prepared agendas avoided the dangers of spontaneity and was readily and smoothly instituted as a customary control measure in his interaction with therapist and analyst alike. Ambiguous and incomplete accounts of experiences and the absence of childhood recollections prompted the therapist to try to order his patient's narratives in accordance with an oedipal paradigm. His interventions afforded the patient direction and relief. The method of communication established in childhood was confirmed in the therapy. In the analysis, the exploration and interpretation of this repetitive mode of communication served to establish an analytic alliance and to modify the patient's pattern of defense.

As a part of such early patterns, the perception and processing of information may exhibit gross and subtle varieties of distortion, in identification and compliance with early caretakers. What is included and what is left out of perception and thought may be attuned to subtle cues in the relationship. In the first case, the disavowal of affect, memory, and fantasy about the death of her father is a clear example of a such a learned mode of perception and processing, and its engagement in the conversion to analysis was a powerful instrument for change. In the second case, the programmed approach to life provided by the patient's father served as a substitute for the patient's own perceptions and functions, seriously interfering with the exploration of problems and their solution. A formula for behavior substituted for spontaneity in perception and thought. This pattern was essentially reenacted in the transference. The problem was identified and engaged from the beginning of the analysis as a crucial issue in establishing an alliance and coping with conflict.

In an elegant statement about the distinctions between therapy and analysis, Stone referred in passing to "the conditions of analysis that provide a basis for the possibility of radical new discovery for the patient and the analyst" (Panel, 1954, p. 165).

As in any voyage of discovery, attention to available maps, appropriate instruments, accumulated lore, and the quality of participation of the explorers is essential to the purpose of the expedition in achieving its goals and maximizing the scientific yield. The historical review with which this paper opens describes the remarkable changes in theory and technique that have accompanied clinical explorations. Creating the conditions for an analysis has included an increasingly sophisticated awareness of the significant elements entering into the analytic situation, thereby adding a scientific aspect to the art of analysis. In the context of those conditions, the analytic process offers the potential for discovery. If the purpose of the treatment is only the application of acquired knowledge, then it is applied psychoanalysis, a form of psychotherapy. The purview of the analyst extends to the whole range of development in his patient and what it evokes in him, with the deliberate purpose of engaging the full richness of each encounter as a unique experience.

REFERENCES

Bernstein, S. B. (1983). Treatment preparatory to psychoanalysis. *J. Amer. Psychoanal. Assn.,* 31:363–390.

Gill, M. M. (1954). Psychoanalysis and exploratory psychotherapy. *J. Amer. Psychoanal. Assn.,* 2:771–797.

Greenson, R. R. (1967). *The Technique and Practice of Psychoanalysis.* New York: Int. Univ. Press.

Kernberg, O. F., et al. (1972). *Bull. Menninger Clin.,* 36:1–275.

Levine, H. B. (1985). Psychotherapy as the initial phase of psychoanalysis. *Int. Rev. Psychoanal.,* 12:285–297.

Panel (1953a). The Essentials of Psychotherapy as Viewed by the Psychoanalyst, O. S. English, Reporter. *J. Amer. Psychoanal. Assn.,* 1:550–561.

Panel (1953b). The Traditional Psychoanalytic Technique and its Variations, E. R. Zetzel, Reporter. *J. Amer. Psychoanal. Assn.,* 1:526–537.

Panel (1954). Psychoanalysis and Dynamic Psychotherapy—Similarities and Differences, Leo Rangell, Reporter. *J. Amer. Psychoanal. Assn.,* 2:152–166.

Panel (1979). Conceptualizing the Nature of the Therapeutic Action of Psychoanalytic Psychotherapy, S. J. Nemetz, Reporter. *J. Amer. Psychoanal. Assn.,* 27:127–144.

Panel (1987). Conversion of Psychotherapy to Psychoanalysis, C. P. Fisher, Reporter. *J. Amer. Psychoanal. Assn.,* 35:713–726.

Schlessinger, N. & Robbins, F. P. (1983). *A Developmental View of the Psychoanalytic Process: Follow-up Studies and their Consequences.* New York: Int. Univ. Press.

Shapiro, D., Jafffe, D., et al. (1981). Survey of Psychoanalytic Practice, 1976: A Summation Distributed by the Amer. Psychoanal. Assn.

Wallerstein, R. (1983). Change agents in adulthood. Presented as a plenary address at Michael Reese Hospital Department of Psychiatry Conference on "The Creativity and Challenges of the Adult Experience," Chicago, March 19, 1983.

Zetzel, E. (1965). The Theory of Therapy in Relation to a Developmental Model of the Psychic Apparatus. *Int. J. Psychoanal.,* 46:39–52.

35 East Wacker Drive
Suite 3200
Chicago, IL 60601

The Fundamental Rule: Its Utilization in the Conversion of Psychoanalytic Psychotherapy to Psychoanalysis

DAVID I. JOSEPH, M.D.

> *So say whatever goes through your mind. Act as though, for instance, you were a traveller sitting next to the window of a railway carriage and describing to someone inside the carriage the changing views which you see outside. Finally, never forget that you have promised to be absolutely honest, and never leave anything out because, for some reason or other, it is unpleasant to tell it.*
>
> Freud (1913, p. 135)

ALTHOUGH ANALYSTS DIFFER REGARDING which factors are essential to psychoanalysis, free association is generally agreed to be a central aspect of the psychoanalytic process. Since Freud (1912) formally articulated the "fundamental rule," analysts have presented it to their patients in a variety of ways, stressing that, without censorship or editing, the analysand should attempt to put into words whatever comes to his mind and whatever he experiences. This paper explores the origins and purpose of fundamental rule in psychoanalysis with particular consideration of its role in the treatment of individuals whose psychoanalytic psychotherapy is converted to psychoanalysis. The manner in

Dr. Joseph is the Associate Director of the Psychiatry Residency Program, St. Elizabeth's Hospital.

which the therapist conceptualizes and presents the fundamental rule will be shown to have important ramifications for the evolution of the transference, for psychoanalytic technique, and for the learning that occurs during the psychoanalytic process.

Psychotherapy and Psychoanalysis

Because my major focus is the conversion of psychotherapy to psychoanalysis, a brief consideration of the difference between the two modes of treatment is necessary as background. I use the term psychoanalytic psychotherapy for those psychotherapies also referred to as insight-oriented, dynamic, or expressive psychotherapy; they are based on a psychoanalytic understanding of the patient and utilize psychoanalytic techniques are used to achieve therapeutic goals through increased self-awareness. Psychoanalytic psychotherapy differs from nonanalytic psychotherapies, such as cognitive/behavioral psychotherapy, which are based on a different conceptualization of the patient's psychopathology, and which employ nonpsychoanalytic techniques. It differs as well from psychoanalysis, which is based on the same understanding of the patient and utilizes the same therapeutic techniques in a treatment characterized by less therapeutic structure, greater fluidity of thought and affect, and by broader therapeutic goals. Historically, the importance and the controversy, especially among American psychoanalysts (I am not sure it has been as important elsewhere) regarding the differences between psychoanalytic psychotherapy and psychoanalysis is highlighted by the fact that the first three volumes of the *Journal of the American Psychoanalytic Association* included no less than 3 Panels (1953, 1954, 1955) on the subject as well as 5 articles (Eissler, 1953; Alexander, 1954; Bibring, 1954; Fromm-Reichmann, 1954; Gill, 1954). These and subsequent articles (Gitelson, 1951; Wallerstein, 1969; Sachs, 1979; Rangell, 1981; Gill, 1984) and yet another Panel (1987) have explored the subject from a variety of perspectives including historical development, patient selection, frequency of sessions, use of the couch, goals of treatment, and psychotherapeutic techniques. To frame this discussion of the conversion of psychoanalytic psychotherapy to psychoanalysis, the amount of structure provided in the treatment and the degree of therapeutic neutrality merit greater elaboration.

Michels (Panel, 1979) has compared the psychotherapist with an "engineer" or guide, as contrasted with the psychoanalyst who is more like a "naturalist," an explorer without any charts for guidance. Ticho (Panel, 1987) has conveyed the same distinction, noting that in expressive psychotherapy "The therapist helps the patient to select areas of exploration by keeping the patient's transference, life situation, and treatment goals under continuous scrutiny" (p. 718). Whereas in psychoanalysis the patient pursues the goal of free association in compliance with the fundamental rule, in psychoanalytic psychotherapy, the patient engages in "free communication" (Bibring, 1954) and participates in a "free interview" (Wallerstein, 1969), terms that suggest a style of communication similar to but more contained than free association. There are differences between the two therapies in the modes of listening as well. Whereas evenly hovering attention characterizes the mode of listening of the psychoanalyst, the psychotherapist must listen with a more narrowly focused state of mind. Leavy (Panel, 1971) has pointed out that "There exists in the analyst's mind a readiness and also an activity, to allow statements to be dissolved, imaginal units to be fragmented and then to be reconstituted in new syntheses" (p. 108). Independent of the patient's mode of communicating, in psychotheraphy the ability to achieve this degree of psychological mobility is limited by a more focused role, less frequent sessions, and by looking at the patient.

The mode of the patient's verbalizations, the mode of the therapist's listening, and the degree of focus provided by the therapist act in concert with the frequency of sessions and the use of the couch or chair to produce the degree of structure that characterizes the therapy. Psychic structure refers to mental mechanisms with a slow rate of change and is responsible for the delay in the expression of impulse that characterizes maturation (Rapoport, 1960). Psychotherapeutic structure regulates the rate of change of the thoughts and feelings the patient expresses and the degree to which the therapist can associate freely in response to his own experience.

While there are differences between psychoanalytic psychotherapy and psychoanalysis, analytic listening characterizes both therapies. As Sachs (1979) emphasizes:

> In psychoanalytic psychotherapy associations are used as much as possible, but the procedure of free association cannot be used. Instead, the therapist creates an atmosphere neutral to conflict while encouraging associations. The insight gained in this way makes psychoanalytic psychotherapy unique among all dynamic psychotherapies. . . . The psychoanalytically oriented therapist functions in the same way in both therapies, creating a continuum in the way he works in the different forms of psychoanalytic psychotherapy (p. 140).

This is in keeping with the fact that "The theory of psychoanalytic therapy and of the psychopathology toward which it is directed is the theory of psychoanalysis" (Rangell, 1981, p. 684).

A continuum also characterizes the degree of the analyst's therapeutic neutrality in psychoanalytic psychotherapy and psychoanalysis. Poland (1984) has distinguished between neutrality as a concept connoting the absence of color and neutrality as a concept reflecting relationships among conflicting or competing forces. To these definitions he adds a third, specifically psychoanalytic concept of neutrality, namely,

> the analyst's neutralization and mastery of his own internal processes. To maintain this self-mastery for the sake of the analysis, the analyst monitors his personal inner world. . . . This provides the basic rule for the analyst, equal in import and coinciding with that for the patient: the analyst must consider and examine *all* experiences within himself in relation to the analysis for all informational value, accepting as data for

> evaluation all observations including those that arise within himself, never ignoring or dismissing anything out of hand [pp. 284–285].

Neutrality also refers to the establishment of a psychological position equidistant from the id, ego, and superego, from internal and external objects, from transference and a focus on original objects, from both sides of the patient's ambivalence, from verbal and nonverbal communication, and from cognitive and empathic modes of perception. As an attitude and a manner of perceiving, responding to, and understanding the patient's associations and communications, neutrality fosters the development of and sustains evenly hovering attention, which is the analyst's equivalent of the patient's free associations. Its "aim is to avoid foreclosure on the analysand's freedom of expression and association" (Schwartz, 1988, p. 418). Kris (1982) has noted that the "analyst must be certain of his compassionate neutrality in order to be *free* (italics mine) to take energetic interpretive measures at one point and to be patiently silent the next" (p. 38). Free association characterizes communication between analysand and analyst freed from the patient's conscious censorship, freed from the constraints imposed by nontherapeutic communications, and less encumbered by the degree of structure that characterizes psychoanalytic psychotherapy. The fundamental rule addresses the expression of unedited thoughts and feelings, but the patient's ability to associate freely is strongly influenced by the analyst's essential neutrality.

Since the psychotherapist focuses the therapy to a greater extent than the psychoanalyst, his position will be characterized by less "neutrality."[1] This "compromise" of neutrality need not constitute a barrier to the conversion of psychoanalytic psychotherapy to psychoanalysis. If the psychotherapist has maintained a consistent

[1]I do not mean to imply that psychotherapy has established goals where psychoanalysis does not, nor that the psychotherapist has a stake in the result of the treatment, whereas the psychoanalyst is indifferent to the outcome of the analytic work. As Poland (1984) has stressed, "no matter his dedication to scientific research, if the analyst's work has no impact on his analysand, the analysis is meaningless" (p. 287).

"analytic attitude" (Schafer, 1983) and "non-directive spirit," (Gill, 1954) the nature of the relationship between patient and psychotherapist will not preclude a complete elucidation and resolution of the transference. Put another way, for the conversion to be successful, the transference developed in the psychotherapy must not have become so rigidly fixed to prevent the fluidity that is essential to psychoanalysis. When technical interventions, such as role-playing, advice-giving, self-disclosure, and meeting with family members have significantly affected the transference, referral to another analyst is usually preferable.

Any number of clinical situations might warrant the conversion of psychoanalytic psychotherapy to psychoanalysis. Realistic factors initially may make psychoanalysis impractical or impossible. Patients initially unable to utilize the analytic method and/or tolerate the analytic situation progress during psychotherapy to where they can utilize and/or tolerate it. The patient's internal conflicts interfere with the ability to make the commitment to psychoanalysis (Weil, 1973; Bernstein, 1983). Psychoanalytic psychotherapy reaches an impasse, necessitating a change in its structure. The patient's initial goals for psychoanalytic psychotherapy become supplanted by other goals for which psychoanalysis is better suited. The psychotherapist (or patient) is consistently unable to make a psychodynamic formulation, which might suggest that analysis would provide the additional data necessary for clarification.

Although analytic parlance usually advances the concept of "converting" psychoanalytic psychotherapy into psychoanalysis, this term is not, in my opinion, the most apt. "Conversion" implies a dramatic change or transformation that will not, if an analytic atmosphere has been maintained throughout the psychotherapy, describe the difference between the two treatments. From a theoretical perspective it seems more accurate to conceptualize the change as a transition rather than a conversion, a distinction that carries a number of implications and is of particular importance when considering the fundamental rule. From a clinical perspective, it seems preferable to explain the reasons for the specific changes entailed in the transition and to avoid altogether naming the "new" therapy as psychoanalysis. Patients who equate the use of the couch with psychoanalysis may often feel quite differently about psychoanalysis as compared with psychotherapy. Some bring to psychoanalysis a preconception that it connotes more severe psychopathology; some consider it a better form of psychotherapy and experience themselves as narcissistically ennobled by virtue of being "in analysis." Psychologically sophisticated individuals may be reassured that they are analyzable.

I would suggest that the term psychoanalysis be reserved for "metatherapeutic" discussions in the same way that ego, id, and superego belong to the vocabulary of metapsychology and have no place in the day-to-day practice of clinical psychoanalysis. Given my identity as a psychoanalyst, my own recommendation is difficult for me to follow, but I do believe that adhering to this course would benefit patients. An alternative would be to include all psychoanalytic therapies in a single category, a position that would prematurely foreclose continuing exploration of how one psychoanalytic treatment differs from another. Regardless of whether one refers to the "new" therapy as psychoanalysis, it is important to provide a careful explanation of how the use of the couch, the increased frequency of sessions, and the utilization of the fundamental rule are responses to a clinical situation that made the changes desirable.

The Fundamental Rule

An understanding of the ways in which the method of free association can be introduced to the analysand is greatly facilitated by a historical review of the development of the fundamental rule. Freud's initial work with hysterical patients used hypnosis to facilitate the recall of traumatic memories and the concurrent release of stangulated affect. The movement from the therapeutic techniques of hypnosis to clinical psychoanalysis and the evolution of a "fundamental rule" occurred gradually, but the concept of the fundamental rule, described in 1900 and formulated in 1912, remained deeply rooted in the relationship between the hypnotist and his subject. The obligatory nature of the patient's responsibility in psychoanalysis is explicitly apparent in Freud's early descriptions of his instructions to the patient (1900, 1913). Lewin (1955) has pointed out that Freud's education and preparation of the patient reflected the anatomic preparation of a patient for hypnosis. Kanzer (1972) has suggested that the requirement by the analyst that the patient comply with the fundamental rule can be linked with the hypnotist's command that the hypnotized patient "remember." From this point of view, the commands of the hypnotist and the elaboration of the fundamental rule by the psychoanalyst are both intended to assist the patient to overcome resistances which he raises to the verbal expression of id derivatives.

Although the relationship between hypnosis and the fundamental rule is central to a historical understanding of the development of the method of free association, the fundamental rule itself, in conjunction with the use of the couch, the frequency and length of analytic sessions, the analyst's neutrality, and the analyst's manner of listening and responding is a derivative of the *process* of inducing the hypnotic trance and is not directly derived from the command that the hypnotized patient remember. Freud (1904) emphasized that "it depends upon the choice of the patient whether he can be hypnotized or not, no matter what the skill of the physician may be" (p. 250). One cannot command an individual to enter a hypnotic trance; one can only instruct the patient what procedures to follow, which, with the hypnotist's assistance, will facilitate the development of a hypnotic state of consciousness. The hypnotist's command to remember is effective only after the state of hypnosis has been induced. As Lewin (1955, p. 198) has said, "To fall back on Freud's old comparison of hypnosis and chloroform anesthesia, it is what one does after the patient is chloroformed that matters most, and this is what we call technique and not situation."

To monitor and regulate the patient's state of consciousness is one of the analyst's most important tasks. Freud (1900) drew the analogy between free association and the state of consciousness that precedes sleep. Lewin says, "coincidental with all other effects of the analyst's remarks, or perhaps even of his presence, there is a deep effect which I [have] likened to the musical: the analyst continuously operates either to wake the patient somewhat or to put him to sleep a little, to soothe or to arouse; and this effect may be quite unconscious for both subject and analyst" (1955, p. 193). Free association Loewenstein once said, establishes a "situation in which multiple meanings appear more clearly and which is closer to poetry than scientific language" (Panel, 1971, p. 109). The method of free association, in concert with the "extrinsic criteria" (Gill, 1954, 1984) of analysis, assists the patient to attain a modified state of consciousness characterized by a greater fluidity of cognition and affect that facilitates recall, understanding, and insight.

In both hypnosis and psychoanalysis, the patient's state of consciousness may change significantly after the treatment has begun. If induction procedures are continued with a person who has entered a hypnotic state the trance may deepen, in which case the "induction procedures are transitional . . . between levels of hypnosis rather than between the waking state and hypnosis." (Hilgard, 1965, p. 23). Similarly, psychoanalytic interventions that reduce the analysand's unconscious resistance to associating freely modify his state of mind in the direction of ever greater mobility of thought and emotion.

The impact of ego psychology shifted attention away from a direct focus on drives and their derivatives and emphasized analysis of the patient's resistance to the perception, experience, and verbalization of id derivatives. This change in the theory of psychoanalytic treatment had significant implications for the concept of a fundamental rule and ramifications for the way analysts could formulate that rule to their patients. As Loewenstein put it, "It needed to be presented no longer as a rigid rule for the patient to obey, but rather as a gradual introduction to the peculiarities of the analytic process" (Panel, 1971, p. 102). Although it would be reasonable to expect that analysts have abandoned the promulgation of a fundamental rule, a concept more applicable to id than ego psychology, a recent study by Lichtenberg and Galler (1987) of the current usage of the fundamental rule indicates the degree to which the concept of a rule, with all its superego ramifications and the attendant parental (discplinarian) behaviors persists. While many analysts indicated a wish to avoid an authoritarian stance in the presentation of the method of free association, an impressive number directly or implicitly took a position very close to that described by Freud in 1912.

Gray (1982) has addressed the question of why developments in psychoanalytic technique have not kept pace with developments in the analytic theory of ego psychology. He mentions Strachey (1934) as one whose important contribution to the understanding of resistance was not accompanied by a similar adaptation in his psychoanalytic technique. A similar difference between expressed theory and technique can be observed in the work of Kanzer (1972) who speaks of the need to "enforce" the fundamental rule, while at the same time arguing that "the essential aim of an interpretation is to disarm the resistances that oppose adherence to the fundamental rule" (p. 256). In his discussion, Gray emphasizes that it

> "is likely that therapeutic action by internalization comes about in many valuable analyses, but to consider this as the ultimate therapeutic factor for *all* analyses significantly limits the development of a technical approach which could offer greater opportunity to many patients for more autonomous ego growth. . . .
>
> I suggest that the essential cognitive and experiential factors involved in such an analysis of neurotic conflict can conveniently be categorized and understood within the concept of *learning process*. This is cognitive process, in respect to the patient's *comprehension* of the analyst's observations concerning the ego and id aspects of the neurotic conflicts; an experi-

ential process in respect to the patient's discovery that his ego can *tolerate and control* the increments of drive derivatives.

Although some patients pathologically and defensively react more than others to the analyst with incorporations, probably all show some regressive tendency in this direction. To the extent that the analyst presents himself through his remarks in an authoritative or parentlike manner, the nonincorporative learning modes of acquiring insight are significantly compromised."

The imposition of an *obligation* to say what comes to mind or a *promise* to follow a fundamental rule interferes with the achievement of the very sense of autonomy that is a central goal of any psychoanalysis. The superego aspects inherent in the concept of a rule and the roles attendant upon both analyst (enforcer) and analysand (submissive follower or oppositional rebel) when such a relationship is established are antithetical to the nondirective spirit which is basic to the analytic process and interfere with the development of the autonomy that is essential to the growth of the patient's ability for self-analysis.

Case Example

Although the concept of a transition more properly describes the movement from psychoanalytic psychotherapy to psychoanalysis, the changes in the nature of psychotherapeutic work can be dramatic. This is reflected in the following case example.

Mrs. W was 26 years old when she sought psychotherapy because of marked anxiety, depression, and suicidal ideation. Her symptoms had started some eight months earlier, following a move to Washington, had grown more severe over the ensuing months, and became particularly intense after the birth of her second child (her first son). When her husband left town on business, her anxiety and suicidal thoughts became extremely frightening, she went to an emergency room and was referred for treatment. A similar episode, which occurred three years before when she had moved with her husband away from her home town, resolved spontaneously. She had had no previous psychotherapy.

Mrs. W always felt unable to compete effectively with her sister who was four years older, her father's favorite, and a very successful student. The patient's mother had a number of miscarriages between the birth of her two children, and the patient was intended to be a boy. At the age of three and a half she was twirling a yo-yo while her father was reading a newspaper, ignoring her. The yo-yo hit him in the face, breaking his glasses, and she recalls his pulling down her pants and beating her with his belt while her mother implored him to stop. The patient vowed never to kiss him again, and apparently didn't until the summer before his sudden death by a myocardial infarction when she was nine. When told of his death, she locked herself in her room and cried alone. From that time on, she "changed" in ways she found difficult to describe, but which reflected an intense bitterness and sense of guilt. She started treatment with very few memories of her father whom she only recalled as a cruel man who hated her.

Mrs. W finished college and completed graduate studies in history. She was married at 20 and described her husband as a very bright, sarcastic, intimidating man. The couple had two children, a girl and a boy.

The patient's mother, a beautiful woman, suffered the loss of her own mother when she was six, after which she was raised by an aunt while her siblings remained with the father. When the patient was three, her mother became depressed and, following the death of Mrs. W's father, became psychotic. Although much improved, she continued to be somewhat paranoid and disorganized. The patient's father, a high school science teacher, was obsessive, distant, and demanding and was very much invested in the academic achievements of his older daughter. Before his death, the family had been very close.

When I first saw her, Mrs. W was distraught, very frightened, tearful and felt overwhelmed; when in the throes of panic, she harbored active suicidal thoughts. She had difficulty coping with her two young children and was often hopeless or despondent. After several hours in close succession, her anxiety and depression decreased, and she began twice-a-week psychoanalytic psychotherapy. This frequency reflected both her need to be with her infant son and the constraints of my schedule. Themes of anger with her mother for being unavailable after her father's death were central in the therapy and were accompanied by much guilt. The wish for approval, fears of being suggestible and easily controlled, and guilt over her intense competition with her sister were also prominent. Mrs. W resorted to a great deal of denial and angrily insisted that her marriage was excellent and ought not to be explored. She bitterly decried the fact that she had not been "invited" to her father's funeral and expressed feelings of being cheated by his early death. Apart from the "yo-yo incident", she remained virtually without specific memories of him.

After two years of psychoanalytic psychotherapy, the patient began coming four times per week and using the couch. The transition from psychotherapy to psychoanalysis was based on several factors. In the months preceding the beginning of analysis she often expressed the sense of being "stuck," and I felt that the work was becoming bogged down and repetitive. Although she did not know what more to talk about, she was still anxious, insecure, and often depressed. Material from these hours suggested that a slow accumulation of highly charged transference material was primarily responsible for the therapeutic impasse. The transition to the use of the couch, the increase in the frequency of hours, and the information that her treatment would be most helpful if she tried without censorship to say whatever came to mind and whatever she experienced were intended to reduce the structure of the therapy and to allow the transference to be experienced, verbalized, tolerated, and worked through.

Once the decision to recommend psychoanalysis had been made, the advisability of referring the patient to another analyst was considered. This woman's psychotherapy had been analytically oriented. The focus of the work had been the clarification and understanding of unconscious conflict. When transference interfered with the flow of material it had been the focus of attention. Aspects of my life had not been revealed, medication had not been prescribed, and overall I felt that neither the length nor the nature of her psychotherapy would prevent the development and resolution of a transference neurosis.

Mrs. W's analysis, which lasted three years (when the family moved away), was punctuated by repeated threats to quit and two "terminations," which she set but ultimately decided against. In the third hour, she had a dream in which she was mutilating a group of people and then putting them back together, and the first year of analytic work was characterized primarily by her intense negative transference. I was perceived as a cold, hateful, mocking man who scorned her affection and laughed at her pain. Her abusive impulses toward me were accompanied by fears that she would get out of control and, because of my size, hurt me seriously. Her biting attacks were interrupted by hours characterized by "stubborn isolation." Memories of feeling "humiliated" at not having a father and fears of having "poisoned" him by withholding her affection led to a dream in which she is naked, playing baseball with two old boyfriends. Her bat is a bent stick, the crowd laughs, and she runs off into a swamp. Several hours later she reported a latency wish to be a professional singer. She also recalled a memory from age three and a half in which she was dancing to attract the attention of a lifeguard and became infuriated when he paid no attention to her.

The recall of this material and the intense negative transference came as a genuine shock to her and were accompanied by marked reduction in her anxiety and depression. Subsequent work led to the recall of many positive memories of father and the consolidation of a highly charged positive transference. This condensed summary reflects the rapid and dramatic changes in the nature of her treatment following the change from psychoanalytic pyschotherapy to psychoanalysis.

Discussion

To avoid an authoritarian position and to clarify the rationale of free association, it is important not to present the method of free association as a fundamental rule. With patients in psychoanalytic psychotherapy, one can indicate that their treatment will be most effective if they discuss whatever is important to them. This procedure encourages considerable freedom without specifically introducing the concept of free association. Given the greater degree of structure in psychoanalytic psychotherapy, it is often difficult, though by no means impossible, to achieve the fluidity that characterizes the state of freely associating. With patients beginning psychoanalysis, or making the transition from psychoanalytic psychotherapy to psychoanalysis, I (like one respondent to Lichtenberg & Galler) limit my comments to a brief statement such as, "Your treatment will be most helpful if you try to put into words whatever you experience or whatever comes to mind." In addition, it is useful to provide a short explanation of how this unstructured ordering of material, along with the increased frequency of sessions and use of the couch, is intended to bring unconscious material to awareness, thereby allowing for analytic understanding, insight, conflict resolution, and growth. This approach avoids the difficulties inherent in an obligation and emphasizes that psychoanalysis, like any other treatment (medical or psychological), is most likely to be successful if the patient understands and follows the recommended components of the therapy. When presented in this fashion the patient's inevitable reluctance and resistance to the method of free association and his sense of being forced to say what comes to mind can be explored from the perspective of the distortion he has introduced and from the point of view that the patient is negating the effectiveness of the treatment whose rationale he has understood.

This manner of introducing free association is educational. Having reviewed the responses to their questionnaire regarding the fundamental rule, Lichtenberg and Galler (1987) also recommend an educational approach to the fundamental rule, but they suggest that the analyst's comments be quite broad and include the following: "(1) a formal statement of explanation of what the analysand is to experience, observe, and verbalize; (2) an explicit suggestion that, in addition to their thoughts, feelings, bodily sensations, images, dreams, and references to the analyst should be verbalized; (3) an explanation that all patients, despite their best efforts, will inevitably experience reluctance to reveal their associations, but these resistances in themselves provide an opportunity for analytic exploration" (p. 72). I believe that, although useful in educating the analysand about psychoanalysis, the introduction of these recommendations will cause sufficient distortion of the transference to outweigh the benefits that might accrue from their use. It seems unnecessary to specify what the patient is to observe and verbalize or to encourage him to pay attention to any particular aspect of his emotional or cognitive experience. One can expect that in the course of an analysis each of the areas identified by Lichtenberg and Galler will be experienced, including the preverbal and presymbolic experience of patients with more immature mental organizations. When the absence of the spontaneous reporting of such material or experience achieves sufficient prominence, it will become apparent to the analyst and can be identified with the goal of understanding the meaning of its absence in the patient's associations. The list of important areas that merit attention will vary to some degree from analyst to analyst. Any short list will be too restricted; any "inclusive" list will be so long as to be self-defeating. In addition to running the risk of affecting the patient's spontaneity, directing his attention to specific areas may unnecessarily introduce issues of pleasing (or displeasing) and following (or rebelling against) the analyst. It seems equally unnecessary to educate the patient about resistance. Not only may such an explanation be experienced as infantilizing, but a formal explanation about resistance may result in the patient's verbalizing material about which he is anxious, ashamed, embarrassed, or guilty, without verbalizing this aspect of his experience. An introduction to psychoanalysis can be educational without being directive or prescriptive.

Freud (1923) wanted to "find the path leading to what had been forgotten or fended off" (p. 238). He expected that this method would demonstrate "that everything that occurred to a patient setting out from a particular starting-point must also stand in an internal connection with that starting-point; hence arose the technique of *educating* [italics mine] the patient to give up the whole of his critical attitude and of making use of the material which was thus brought to light for the purpose of uncovering the connections that were being sought" (p. 238). By providing an initial understanding of how the therapeutic situation and free association are intended to facilitate the achievement of the goals of the analysis, an educational introduction makes it more likely that the decision to begin psychoanalysis and to pursue free association will be based on shared understanding and will not primarily reflect compliance with a transference figure who has promulgated a fundamental rule that must be followed.

All psychoanalyses involve a transition from one type of psychotherapy to another. The patient who "begins" his treatment with psychoanalysis has, in fact, made the transition from a very brief psychotherapy, namely, the psychoanalytic evaluation to psychoanalysis. This transition, like the transition from psychoanalytic psychotherapy to psychoanalysis, is recommended when the specific therapeutic situation of analysis is necessary to bring into awareness the "regressive manifestations" (Gill, 1984) of the patient's mental functioning which heretofore have been in disguise. As Arlow (1975) has said, "the oft-repeated statement that psychoanalytic technique induces regression in the patient . . . is a principle which has been quoted and circulated without challenge for a long time. It seems to me that what the psychoanalytic situation does is to create an atmosphere, a set of conditions, which permit regressive aspects of the patient's mental functioning, long present, to reemerge in forms that are clearer and easier to observe" (p. 73). Rules, unnecessary instructions, and explicit recommendations regarding the areas of proper analytic scrutiny represent iatrogenic contributions to the analytic atmosphere which may limit the fluidity of the analysis and encourage a transference more dominated by superego factors than would otherwise be the case. Providing an explanation for the frequency of sessions, the use of the couch, and especially for free association, will facilitate the transition to psychoanalysis and will clarify how these changes are intended to allow patient and analyst to gain access to material previously unavailable in the psychotherapeutic situation despite the best efforts of each.

REFERENCES

Alexander, F. (1954). Psychoanalysis and psychotherapy. *J. Amer. Psychoanal. Assn.*, 2:722–733.

Arlow, J. (1975). Discussion of paper by M. Kanzer. "The Therapeutic and Working Alliances." *Int. J. Psychoanalytic Psychother.*, 4:69–73.

Bernstein, S. W. (1983). Treatment preparatory to psychoanalysis. *J. Amer. Psychoanal. Assn.*, 31:363–390.

Bibring, E. (1954). Psychoanalysis and the dynamic psychotherapies. *J. Amer. Psychoanal. Assn.*, 2:745–770.

Eissler, K. P. (1953). The effect of the structure of the ego on psychoanalytic technique. *J. Amer. Psychoanal. Assn.*, 1:104–143.

Freud, S. (1900). The interpretation of dreams. *S.E.*, 4 & 5.

_____ (1904). Freud's psychoanalytic procedure. *S.E.*, 7.

_____ (1912). The dynamics of the transference. *S.E.*, 12.

_____ (1913). The beginning of treatment. *S.E.*, 12.

_____ (1923). Two encyclopedia articles. *S.E.*, 18.

Fromm-Reichmann, F. (1954). Psychoanalytic and general dynamic conceptions of theory and of therapy: differences and similarities. *J. Amer. Psychoanal. Assn.*, 2:711–721.

Gill, M. M. (1954). Psychoanalysis and exploratory psychotherapy. *J. Amer. Psychoanal. Assn.*, 2:771–797.

_____ (1984). Psychoanalysis and psychotherapy: A revision. *Int. Rev. Psychoanal.*, 11:161–178.

Gitelson, M. (1951). Psychoanalysis and dynamic psychiatry. *Arch. Neurol. & Psychiat.*, 66:280–288.

Gray, P. (1982). "Developmental lag" in the evolution of technique for psychoanalysis of neurotic conflict. *J. Amer. Psychoanal. Assn.*, 30:621–656.

Hilgard, E. R. (1965). *The Experience of Hypnosis.* New York, NY: Harcourt, Brace & World.

_____ (1981). Freud's "Analytic pact": The standard therapeutic alliance. *J. Amer. Psychoanal. Assn.*, 26:69–87.

Kanzer, W. (1972). Superego aspects of free association and the fundamental rule. *J. Amer. Psychoanal. Assn.*, 20:69–87.

Kris, A. O. (1982). *Free Association: Method and Process.* New Haven/London: Yale Univ. Press.

Lewin, B. D. (1955). Dream psychology and the analytic situation. *Psychoanal. Q.*, 24:169–199.

Lichtenberg, J. D. & Galler, F. P. (1987). The fundamental rule: A study of current usage. *J. Amer. Psychoanal. Assn.*, 35:47–76.

Panel (1953). Essentials of psychotherapy as viewed by the psychoanalyst. O. S. English, reporter. *J. Amer. Psychoanal. Assn.*, 1:550–551.

Panel (1955). Psychoanalysis and psychotherapy. J. O. Chassell, Reporter. *J . Amer. Psychoanal. Assn.*, 3:528–533.

Panel (1971). The basic rule: Free Association—A Reconsideration. H. Seidenberg, Reporter. *J. Amer. Psychoanal. Assn.*, 19:98–109.

Panel (1979). Conceptualizing the nature of the therapeutic action of psychoanalytic psychotherapy. S. J. Nemetz, Reporter. *J. Amer. Psychoanal. Assn.*, 27:127–144.

Panel (1987). Conversion of Psychotherapy to Psychoanalysis, C. P. Fisher, Reporter. *J. Amer. Psychoanal. Assn.*, 35:713–726.

Poland, W. S. (1984). On the analyst's neutrality. *J. Amer. Psychoanal. Assn.*, 32:283–299.

Rangell, L. (1954). Similarities and differences between psychoanalysis and dynamic psychotherapy. *J. Amer. Psychoanal. Assn.*, 2:734–744.

______ (1981). Psychoanalysis and dynamic psychotherapy: Similarities and differences 25 years later. *Psychoanal. Q.*, 50:665–693.

Rapoport, D. (1967). *The Structure of Psychoanalytic Theory: a Systematizing Attempt. Psycholog. Issues, Monogr.* 2. New York: Int. Univ. Press.

Sachs, D. M. (1979). On the relationship between psychoanalysis and psychoanalytic psychotherapy. *J. Phila. Assn. Psychoanal.*, 6:119–145.

Schafer, R. (1984). *The Analytic Attitude.* New York: Basic Books.

Schwartz, W. (1988). What makes something analytic? *Psychiat.*, 51:417–426.

Strachey, J. (1934). The nature of the therapeutic action of psychoanalysis. *Int. J. Psychoanal.*, 50:117–126.

Wallerstein, R. S. (1969). Introduction to panel on psychoanalysis and psychotherpy. *Int. J. Psychoanal.*, 50:117–126.

Weil, A. P. (1973). Ego strengthening prior to analysis. *Psychoanal. Study Child.*, 28:287–301.

St. Elizabeth's
District of Columbia
Commission of Mental Health Services
Barton Hall
Washington, DC 20032

The Emotional Position of the Analyst in the Shift from Psychotherapy to Psychoanalysis

ALAN Z. SKOLNIKOFF, M.D.

When the question of converting from psychotherapy to psychoanalysis arises, the focus ordinarily is on the patient—especially the patient's capacity or readiness for the change. My focus, in contrast, is on the analyst's state of mind when confronting this circumstance. And because the analyst does live in the real world and is affected by it, it seems reasonable to start with a few observations on the external factors impinging on him or her.

The most conspicuous of these is the change in the general attitude of the public and broad mental health community toward psychoanalysis viewed in comparison to psychotherapy. It is not necessary to compare the current climate of opinion with that of the midcentury when psychoanalysis was the treatment of choice for anyone with the necessary time, money, and patience and when patients undergoing all sorts of therapy referred to their "analyses." We need only compare today's climate with that of a decade or so ago to find differences in the way both analysts and patients feel about analysis.

The general public, prospective patients, and thoughtful people in related disciplines are now questioning whether psychoanalysis

Dr. Skolnikoff is Training and Supervising Analyst, San Francisco Psychoanalytic Institute, and Associate Clinical Professor, Department of Psychiatry, University of California, San Francisco.

is the treatment of choice even for neurotic conditions, long thought to be the special area of our expertise. Candidates today are fewer in number, and those few find it increasingly difficult to acquire the analytic patients they need to order to satisfy their training requirements.

Have these changes actually influenced shifts in conceptualization in the literature? Is there, for example, a new tendency to blur the distinction between borderline, narcissistic, and neurotic pathology so as to permit us to include all these categories as suitable for analytic treatment? In England the notion that borderline patients are treated in analysis finds general acceptance. Because neurotic patients are hard to come by (Sandler & Sandler, 1984), patients who have addictions, perversions, and chronic physical illness as part of their central pathology are also treated by this modality. Previously, many of these features in the personality of patients that we treat would have been considered absolute contraindications for psychoanalysis. Now, analytic treatment is freely suggested, with a blurring of distinctions of the technical modifications that are made as contrasted with the so-called classical technique that had been applied to neurotic conditions (Eissler, 1953). Psychoanalytic techniques have changed considerably since Eissler's cautious recommendations on the introduction of parameters with patients manifesting specific ego weaknesses.

These external factors influence how the psychoanalytic therapist conceptualizes what he does and whether he considers his work to be analysis or not. And because there is some confusion about what constitutes the essential differences between a psychotherapeutic and a psychoanalytic stance, we often fall back on the form rather than the substance of the treatment. The use of the couch or the frequency of the sessions receives emphasis, rather than the underlying purpose of these devices.

Rangell (1981) shows how the concern for the formal considerations of analysis 25 years ago (the use of the couch, frequency of sessions, and restricting the words of the analyst) was central. He sees his own analytic experience in more flexible terms since then, in that he feels he is able to engage in a psychoanalytic process seeing patients at infrequent intervals for clusters of hours. He emphasizes also that analysis as it is practiced uses manipulation by its very structure—the rule of abstinence and the neutrality of the analyst impose the conditions that bring on the regression and the emergence of the pathology we wish to study.

Gill (1988) also departs from his earlier position. He now sees the analyst as practicing psychoanalysis even if he alters the external circumstances of the situation to a reduced frequency of once or twice a week or use of vis-à-vis instead of the couch. Rather, he sees the primary distinction as the much more frequent use of suggestion in psychotherapy and a predominant focus on understanding the relationship between the analyst and therapist in psychoanalysis. He sees the analytic process as not having an end point. It can only be accomplished to a greater or lesser degree; it is not an all-or-none process.

Freud (1913), as we know, initially decided to use the couch on the presumption that by the patient not facing him and his not reacting to the visual stimulus of the patient's face, free association on the part of the patient could truly be accomplished. He also candidly admitted that to use the couch reduced the self-consciousness that resulted from being stared at all day. It also furthered free-floating attention. It is the *relative* sensory deprivation that occurs without the stimulus of the face-to-face encounter that permits the patient's and the therapist's thoughts more latitude. Stolorow's (see below, this issue) view of the use of the couch as not necessarily ensuring an analytic process should lead us to look more closely at previous assumptions. The use of the couch can serve an analytic process if it enhances the understanding of resistances and improves the focus on ruptures in the free-associative process. Obviously, the lack of mutual stimulation that would be present in the vis-à-vis situation could further focus regressive thought processes. It can also serve to isolate or repress fantasies that would otherwise be stimulated by visual cues. We must remind ourselves that the use of the couch alone is not a substitute for the analytic work. Both patient and analyst can use the couch situation as a way of avoiding and resisting the analytic process. The analyst, with his free-floating attention, may wander far afield from a patient that doesn't stimulate him, satisfying himself with more gratifying thoughts far from anything that relates to the patient. It is easy enough to say that such deviation from thinking about the patient can be noted by the analyst, who eventually tolerates and understands this deviation as meaningful in his reactions to the patient and perhaps explicating a specific interaction which gives a clue to some aspect of the patient's pathology. But this isn't always the case; the analyst might deceive himself into thinking that he is doing analysis when he is actually just marking time. Under the guise of patience, he might for considerable periods remain in a hostile silence to avoid his frustration. The patient may use the couch for similar reasons, to resist the analysis, a form of resistance not always easy to point out. Patients are often enraptured by their free associations and play with them as if they were things in themselves, or they may use the free-associative technique as a way of avoiding the conflicts that they initially came to treatment with.

The same could be said about frequency of treatment. We recommend that a patient be seen at least four times a week for the purpose of carefully following the development of resistances, promoting regression, and developing a vivid transference. But frequency of sessions does not necessarily further an analytic attitude. The patient, regardless of how the analyst explains the reason for the frequency, often sees it as a supportive procedure, even if the analyst is mostly silent and only interprets conflict. What is discussed is not as important as the attitude of patient and analyst toward their respective roles. Here the distinction between the therapist being helpful and the therapist understanding is perhaps one that best defines the distinction between analysis and therapy. Also, what is happening in the psychoanalytic situation has to be experienced as well as understood; that is, in the therapeutic split, which implies that both the patient and analyst can integrate their experience with their observations. Both patient and analyst must have this capacity (Sterba, 1934).

There is a dilemma for the therapist-analyst: most analysts feel that *only* understanding can ultimately be helpful even if transiently painful. Analysts also contrast their work or identities with those of psychiatrists. They associated the latter more with supportive or directive comments and the use of drugs to relieve anxiety and depression. Here the clear distinction of therapist as healer in contrast to the patient as diseased is more prominent than in the analytic situation where both analyst and patient are engaged in trying to understand an interaction. In the analytic situation, an ordeal fantasy predominates. Perhaps this is associated with the long middle phase, which is accompanied by intense transferences—and countertransferences—which, when their origins are understood, will eventually lead to "cure." The ordeal is associated with the experience of the patient-analyst pair transiently (sometimes for long periods) wondering, during periods of intense negative transferences, whether the work of understanding will be helpful. We use the term *negative therapeutic reaction* to describe the abyss that we might fall into in our search for understanding.

Let us suppose, for example, that the patient and analyst discover that the patient had a truly depriving mother. How, if the analyst remains in a truly analytic mode, can he help the patient differentiate the analyst from the transference figure of the depriving mother? Does he not reveal himself or switch roles to that of the "healer" by clearly demonstrating to the patient in a variety of covert ways that he is unlike the depriving mother? Perhaps it is this departure on the part of analysts who focus on disturbed object relations with patients having traumatic backgrounds that accounts for accusations by other analysts, with a different theoretical view that emphasizes drive vicissitudes over object relations, who believe they can maintain an analytic neutrality as they interpret drive conflicts. These latter feel their colleagues have slipped into offering the more comfortable but less analytic "corrective emotional experience."

The interface of therapy and analysis, or the therapeutic-analytic split, confronts the analyst at each stage of his career.

Senior colleagues encourage younger colleagues to be ascetic or celibate, but frequently admit to quasi-social interactions with patients, when they rationalize as part of the "real relationship." Lipton (1977) used this term to describe Freud's technique as separate from his relationship with his patients. We speak of the pleasures of the contemplative life. We feel noble that we are able to avoid seduction or interaction with our patients. In our own circles we are proud of our capacity for omniscient silence or unfailing empathy. We see our work egos as leading us to derive pleasure from understanding, and we encourage our patients to do the same. This way of thinking corresponds to the tradition in medicine which holds that the search for diagnosis is the end point of knowledge. Therapeutics are considered merely palliative, dealing only with symptoms rather than "understanding" the underlying disease. Again, focusing on the form rather than the substance is not as important as the difference in the attitudes of the patient and analyst to the process.

The differences between therapy and analysis become clear when we look at the therapist-patient duo and the mutual understanding about what they are doing, separately and together. I am talking about their conscious as well as unconscious perceptions and motives. We all know of therapist-patient pairs who feel they are engaged with the patient on the couch, engaging in free association, and the analyst interpreting conflicts and resistances and their transference manifestations. However, the patient may see the therapist's primary activity as direct support and encouragement. The ordeal of self-and-other exploration and the ensuing regressive negative transferences and resistances, which don't easily yield to interpretation, is essentially avoided because it is too painful or frustrating.

We must distinguish what in the psychoanalytic situation itself is supportive (primordial transference [Stone, 1961], the fantasy of the silent analyst as being able to listen to and/or tolerate a great deal) from the analyst's actual activity. On a continuum, then, between therapy and analysis, analyst and patient must be more interested in experiencing, observing, and understanding the psychoanalytic situation as it develops than in *doing* something about it. I believe that the capacity for agreement between patient and analyst to conduct psychoanalytic therapy transcends diagnostic categories. It is the mutual capacity to study the fantasied, as-if, played-at, relationship that develops between people when they begin to get to know one another (here I am presuming the patient discovers or fantasizes a great deal about the analyst, as well as the reverse) with the safety (and disappointment as well) of knowing that no real gratification, apart from being understood, will occur.

Two brief clinical examples will demonstrate the complexity of what constitute the essential differences between psychoanalysis and psychotherapy. The first example illustrates a situation in which the patient complied with the form but, in my opinion, was never able to sufficiently engage in a psychoanalytic process as I understand it. He nevertheless achieved from his perspective (and mine) an excellent psychotherapeutic result.

He was in his late thirties and had been briefly married several years before, and now despaired of finding a suitable woman to marry for the purpose of having a family. He had a rigid obsessional character with reaction formations and isolation defenses which concealed sadistic trends. Consciously he presented himself as a somewhat helpless, passive individual who could easily be pushed around. He readily accepted my recommendation for analysis, assuming that analysis would transform him; he had tried other nonanalytic therapies without success.

He readily took to the couch and appeared to be very cooperative. However, despite some sophistication about analysis and the analytic process, he was unable to free-associate and avoided any feelings about me other than viewing me as an ideal helper. On a few occasions he became dramatically angry or disappointed with me, but when I tried to pursue the feelings in ensuing hours, he denied they ever existed. For weeks at a time, he would start sessions with animation; but after listing what he wished to discuss, would rapidly fall asleep for the entire hour. He was unable to discuss what this meant except in rational or moralistic terms.

After three years he became involved with two different women (one younger, pretty, and frivolous, the other older and more serious) and couldn't decide which would be his choice for his ideal mate. He spent months filling the hour with strategies of how he would decide. Finally, with great frustration and some anger, he asked, "Can't you do anything to help me?"

I had long since given up trying to analyze the transference implications of such questions and, in frustration, I responded, "From what you've been saying, you seem to be leaning toward choosing the older one."

He responded dramatically by thanking me effusively. Within the next few months he made some dramatic changes in his life with relative ease and confidence. First he decided to marry the older woman, then he took a prestigious job, and shortly thereafter he impregnated her.

About six months later, after he had accomplished everything he came for (life goals) and I having accomplished nothing (analytic goals) I had intended, he terminated the analysis. He was effusive in his praise of my work with him.

Three years later I encountered him by chance in a hotel where I was attending a conference. He introduced me to his wife and two children; they looked like your ideal happy family. He was now even more effusive in his praise of me to his wife and family.

In giving this example I do not mean to diminish the psychotherapeutic result: I wish to underscore that, although the treatment had the form of analysis, the patient himself did not work analytically.

A second, briefer example illustrates the reverse situation. I have been working with a young married woman in her late twenties once a week for six months. She is functioning on a borderline level with predominantly obsessional defenses; I have been unable to schedule more frequent sessions because of her job-related travels. I'm not sure that she wouldn't regress too severely if more frequent sessions were possible. As it stands, the work follows an analytic framework and she experiences strong erotic or aggressive feelings toward me, is able to reflect about why they are occurring, can hear my interpretations at their manifest level, but can also talk about how she experiences them. She can compare her feelings toward me with those toward her former therapist in another city. She uses an understanding of herself in her intense transference feelings toward me as the major aspect of our work. Despite her fragile ego, she appears to be able to tolerate shifts in her defenses with an awareness of the dangers and rewards. I would not call the work that we are engaged in "analytic," but I think we are engaged in the analytic process.

Why do we analyst choose to analyze rather than do therapy? What is our motive? One has to presume that curiosity, hopefully with considerable sublimination of voyeuristic impulses, operates as a motive to continue the work. But other motives and feelings are awakened as a result, and often determine the analyst's choice of treatment. Solomon (1982), in reviewing the concept of narcissism, points to the need for the analyst to modify grandiose and omnipotent fantasies into attainable goals. An analyst, she says, should not give up his ideals, but rather be aware of the limitations of any given theoretical persuasion. I believe that we analysts, in undertaking our work, are constantly struggling with grandiose fantansies of what we might accomplish. Certainly it is a deprivation always to play a fantasied role. Perhaps this partly accounts for the undue length of many analyses; namely, the patient's, or analyst's, unwarranted expectations of what analysis can accomplish.

We should remember that when we say that we can't analyze something in a patient, we are simultaneously speaking about our own incapacity as well as the patient's. That incapacity is often in the direction of a fantasy that might occur in the analyst, one which might arouse too much anxiety. It is possible that either the patient or the analyst might be frightened of being overwhelmed by aggressive or erotic feelings.

Returning to the subject of conversion: there are many reasons to convert from therapy to analysis or vice versa in addition to the issue of whether or not the patient is analyzable. Bassen (1989) describes some examples of transference-countertransference enactments hidden in the motives of analysts and patients for conversion from therapy to analysis. Frequently these motives can control or redress intense feelings that have developed, rather than further them. Some analysts like seeing patients vis-à-vis, both get a sense of comfort from the arrangement, which the analyst senses will be lost if the patient uses the couch.

In addition to Bassen's clinical illustrations, I wish to mention some other common situations. Sometimes both the patient and analyst agree readily to start the analysis, failing to look at the resistance to a true analytic process that had existed in the vis-à-vis situation. In these circumstances the use of the couch can permit, for example, an obsessional patient to isolate his feelings and to use a variety of words that he wouldn't have been able to use in a vis-à-vis treatment. He might consciously state that he feels more comfortable using the couch, but often isolates this comfort to the couch and doesn't take anything that he learns in the relationship with the analyst to his outside world. All of what he experiences happens only in the analysis. Often the therapist, bored or detached from such a patient, welcomes the hour and uses it to distract himself with pleasant fantasies far removed from the patient. He justifies this departure as based on his need to indulge himself because of how difficult the patient is. Although the analyst theoretically assumes that his work ego will bring this matter to his attention, he frequently justifies and rationalizes his need to be distracted by thinking how the patient would not be able to tolerate an interpretation of his isolation. Here the patient and analyst collude to conduct what appears to have the form of analysis, but certainly not the substance; my extended clinical example of the obsessional male patient contained those elements. Here also the dilemma of tact can go both ways. We believe that we should use tact before we bring up certain areas of conflict that are difficult for the patient, or certain aspects of the negative transference that could be overwhelming. Tact can be used to permit the appropriate dosing of conflictual material, but it can also be used to indefinitely postpone confrontation, with the rationale that certain conflicts can't be dealt with because of the pathology of the patient.

Although I have focused on the misuse of the form of analysis, obviously there are other, nonverbal factors that can be studied through the use of the couch and the frequency of sessions. The lack of stimulation between patient and analyst and the frequency may facilitate the development of silence. There isn't the same pressure for the analyst to talk or to relate directly to the patient because of visual clues. His attention can wander freely to imagine whatever he wishes, with all of the attendant dangers and opportunities. Klauber (1972) suggests that the analyst frequently interprets to escape from the danger of not knowing or from being overwhelmed with incipient strong feelings. The patient, in turn, often experiences the analysis and the analyst's silence as being too teasing, with its "as-if" quality. Not being able to tolerate this, the patient has to make it real by eliciting some reaction from the analyst. It certainly helps if the analyst has a satisfying life in reality as an antidote to the seduction of the fantasied relationship with the patient. Nevertheless, there is always the temptation to make the relationship with the patient more therapeutic than analytic to avoid the pull of the transference-countertransference situation.

In summary, I subscribe to Gill's idea that there is no real dichotomy between psychotherapy and psychoanalysis but rather a continuum. I believe the major factors in the motivation of the analyst-therapist to conduct one type of treatment or another are his emotional reactions to the patient in the analytic-therapeutic situation. The focus on the form of conversion is somewhat misplaced if one considers that the analytic attitude should be the principal point of discussion in determining the nature of treatment.

REFERENCES

Bassen, C. (1989). Transference-countertransference enactment in the recommendation to convert psychotherapy to psychoanalysis.*Int. Rev. Psychoanal.*, 16:79–92.

Eissler, K. (1953). The effect of the structure of the ego on psychoanalytic technique. *J. Amer. Psychoanal. Assn.*, 1:104–193.

______ (1979). A possible endangerment of psychoanalysis in the U.S. *Int. Rev. Psychoanal.*, 6:15–22.

Freud, S. (1913). On beginning of treatment. *S.E.,* 12.

_____ (1919). Lines of advance in psycho-analytic therapy. *S.E.,* 17.

Gill, M. M. (1988). Converting psychotherapy into psychoanalysis. *Contemp. Psychoanal.,* 24:262–274.

Klauber, J. (1972). On the relationship of transference and interpretation in psychoanalytic therapy. *Int. J. Psychoanal.,* 53:385–391.

Lipton, S. D. (1977). Freud's technique as shown in his analysis of the Rat Man. *Int. J. Psychoanal.,* 58:255–273.

Rangell, L. (1981). Psychoanalysis and dynamic psychotherapy: similarities and differences twenty-five years later. *Psychoanal. Q.,* 50:665–693.

Sandler, J., & Sandler, A. M. (1984). The past unconscious, the present unconscious, and interpretation of the transference. *Psychoanal. Inquiry,* 4:367–400.

Solomon, R. Z. (1982). Man's reach. *J. Amer. Psychoanal. Assn.,* 30:325–346.

Sterba, R. (1934). The fate of the ego in analytic therapy. *Int. J. Psychoanal.,* 15:117–126.

Stone, L. C. (1961). *The Psychoanalytic Situation.* New York: Int. Univ. Press.

Wallerstein, R. (1981). The psychoanalyst's life: expectations, vicissitudes, and reflections. *Int. Rev. Psychoanal.,* 8:285–298.

_____ (1986). Forty-two lives in treatment: a study of psychoanalysis and psychotherapy. New York: Guilford.

205 Edgewood Avenue
San Francisco, CA 94117

Converting Psychotherapy to Psychoanalysis: A Critique of the Underlying Assumptions

ROBERT D. STOLOROW, Ph.D.

UNDERLYING ANY CONSIDERATION of the question of converting psychotherapy to psychoanalysis is a set of assumptions about what constitute the defining features that distinguish psychoanalysis from other modes of therapy. In this paper, I examine four such assumptions – or, as I prefer to call them, myths – about the essential nature of a psychoanalytic process.

1. The Myth of the Neutral Analyst

It is widely assumed that one feature distinguishing psychoanalysis from other therapies is the analyst's consistent adherence to a stance of "technical neutrality." Indeed, according to Kernberg (Panel, 1987), it is the degree of the psychotherapist's deviation from technical neutrality that will determine the ease with which successful conversion to psychoanalysis can be achieved: the more neutral the therapist, the easier the shift will be (p. 720). But how is such neutrality to be defined? And does it really exist?

The literature on analytic neutrality is riddled with incongruities

Dr. Stolorow is a member of the faculty of the Southern California Psychoanalytic Institute and a member of the core faculty of the Institute for the Psychoanalytic Study of Subjectivity.

(see Leider, 1983). Often neutrality is equated with Freud's (1915) dictum that "treatment must be carried out in abstinence" (p. 165)—the analyst must not offer his patients any instinctual satisfactions. This technical injunction derives from the theoretical assumption that the primary constellations with which psychoanalysis is concerned are products of repressed instinctual drive derivatives. Gratification, according to this thesis, interferes with the goals of bringing the repressed instinctual wishes into consciousness, tracking their genetic origins, and ultimately achieving their renunciation and sublimation.

But in what sense can this stance of abstinence be said to be neutral? Surely not from the standpoint of the analyst who practices it, because for him abstinence is an expression of the deeply held belief system to which he adheres in conducting his analytic work (Basch, 1983), a belief system that includes basic assumptions about human nature and psychological illness and health.

More important, when one assumes a position from the *patient's* perspective, it is apparent that abstinence—the purposeful frustration of the patient's wishes and needs—could never be experienced by the patient as a neutral stance. Relentless abstinence on the part of the analyst decisively skews the therapeutic dialogue, provoking hostility and tempestuous conflicts that are more an artifact of the therapist's stance than a genuine manifestation of the patient's primary psychopathology (Wolf, 1976; Kohut, 1977). As Stone (1961) and Gill (1984) have pointed out, so-called regressive transference neuroses, thought by many to be a *sine qua non* of an analytic process, may actually be iatrogenic reactions to the indiscriminate application of the principle of abstinence. Thus an attitude of abstinence not only may fail to facilitate the analytic process; it may be inherently inimical to it (Wolf, 1976; Basch, 1983). In an earlier work (Stolorow et al., 1987), my collaborators and I suggested that the rule of abstinence be replaced with the precept that the analyst's interventions should, as much as possible, be guided by an ongoing assessment of what is likely to facilitate or obstruct the unfolding, illumination, and transformation of the patient's subjective world. Such assessments require careful analytic investigation of the specific meanings that the analyst's actions or nonaction come to acquire for the patient.

Closely allied to the rule of abstinence, and also considered by many to be an essential constituent of analytic neutrality, is Freud's (1912) recommendation that the analyst "should be opaque to his patients and, like a mirror, should show them nothing but what is shown to him" (p. 118). As Gill (1984) has pointed out, the assumption that the analyst can remain anonymous denies the essentially interactive nature of the analytic process. Everything the analyst does or says—including most especially the interpretations he offers—are products of his psychological organization, disclosing central aspects of his personality to the patient. These impressions, in turn, are decisive in codetermining the development of the transference. Like the rule of abstinence, the analyst's misguided belief that he can keep his own personality out of the analytic dialogue itself produces transference artifacts that may be countertherapeutic.

A third conception of neutrality, invoked, for example, by Brenner (1976) and Kernberg (Panel, 1987), is Anna Freud's (1936) statement that the analyst "takes his stand at a point equidistant from the id, the ego and the super-ego" (p. 28), a stance that she equates with one of "clear objectivity" and an "absence of bias" (pp. 28–29). Leaving aside the considerable difficulties involved in attempting to measure distances between oneself and hypothetical mental institutions, I wish to emphasize that this concept of neutrality, like the principle of abstinence, is rooted in a theoretical belief system—the tripartite model of the mind—and hence is not unbiased or neutral at all. Interpretations offered from this metaphorical point of equidistance encourage the patient to adopt the analyst's beliefs about the structure of the mind and, to that extent, they are suggestions.

The myth of the neutral analyst has persisted even within psychoanalytic self psychology. Reacting against the equation of neutrality with abstinent unresponsiveness, Kohut (1977) defined analytic neutrality "as the responsiveness to be expected, on an average, from persons who have devoted their life to helping others with the aid of insights obtained via the empathic immersion into their inner life" (p. 252). While I find this a felicitous characterization of the analytic stance, I cannot agree that it describes a neutral one. Like the principles of abstinence and equidistance, it is rooted in a theoretical belief system, albeit one that places the accent on the role of optimal empathic responsiveness in facilitating the development of a healthy self. Furthermore, as Kohut (1980) fully recognized, "a stituation . . . in which one person has committed himself for prolonged periods to extend his 'empathic intention' toward another" (p. 487) is surely not experienced by the patient as a neutral one, meeting as it does his deepest longings to be understood.

Kohut (1980), however, contended that empathy "is in essence neutral and objective" (p. 483), and Wolf (1983) has suggested that Kohut's definition of empathy "implies an attitude of objectivity with regard to the patient's subjectivity" (p. 675). To expect that an analyst can be neutral or objective with respect to his patient's subjectivity, and thereby gaze upon the patient's experience with pure and presuppositionless eyes, is tantamount to requiring the analyst to eliminate his own psychological organization from the analytic system. This, in my view, is an impossible feat, especially when the most powerful expressions of the patient's subjectivity are directed toward the analyst himself—hardly a distinterested party. What the analyst can and should strive for in his self-reflective efforts is awareness of his own personal organizing principles—including those enshrined in his theories—and of how these principles are unconsciously shaping his analytic understandings and interpretations.

If "technical neutrality," however it may be defined, is an illusion, how then is the analyst's stance to be characterized? Following Kohut (1959), my collaborators and I (Stolorow et al., 1987) have argued that the analytic stance is best conceptualized as an attitude of sustained empathic inquiry—an attitude, that is, that consistently seeks to comprehend the meaning of the patient's expressions from a perspective within, rather than outside, the patient's own subjective frame of reference. Like the rule of abstinence, the empathic stance, too, decisively shapes the analytic dialogue, but in an entirely different direction. Sustained empathic inquiry by the analyst contributes to the creation of a therapeutic situation in which the patient increasingly comes to believe that his most profound emotional states and needs can be understood in depth. This, in turn, encourages the patient to develop and expand his own capacity for self-reflection and to persist in articulating ever more vulnerable and sequestered regions of his subjective life. Equally important, it progressively establishes the analyst as an understanding presence with whom early unmet needs can be revived and aborted developmental thrusts reinstated. The attitude of sustained empathic inquiry is thus central in establishing, maintaining, and continually strengthening the selfobject dimension of the transference bond with the analyst (Kohut, 1977, 1984).

2. The Myth of Interpretation Without Suggestion

Following Freud's (1919) distinction between "the pure gold of analysis" and "the copper of direct suggestion" (p. 168), Gill (1988) has declared that "the central technique in a psychoanalytic psychotherapy is to combat symptoms by a relationship, that is by suggestion, while the central technique of psychoanalysis is to analyze the relationship with the purpose of bringing about change . . ." (p. 265). The essential method of psychoanalysis, according to Gill, "is to analyze the transference, to make explicit the transference meaning of suggestion which has been wittingly used and to interpret unwitting suggestion wherever it can be discerned" (p. 271).

Although I agree entirely with Gill's emphasis on the analysis of transference, to my mind the sharp distinction he draws between relationship and suggestion on the one hand and analysis and interpretation on the other creates a false dichotomy, mirroring the long-standing debate over the centrality of affective bonding versus cognitive insight in bringing about change in psychoanalysis

(Friedman, 1978). The analyst's transference interpretations are not disembodied transmissions of insight *about* the analytic relationship. They are an inherent, inseparable component *of* that very bond, and their therapeutic action derives from the nexus of relatedness in which they crystallize (Stolorow et al., 1987). Gill himself has noted (1984) the new relational experience that accompanies the interpretation of transference and has proposed that "cognitive insight into the patient's interpersonal schemata and new affective experience are aspects of a complex whole" (p. 171).

Gill (1984) has also remarked that "every time the analyst intervenes he may be experienced as suggesting a direction for the patient to pursue" (p. 171). I suggest that this truism vitiates the sharp distinction between analysis of transference and suggestion. The commonly held idea that interpretation simply lifts into awareness what lies hidden within the patient is a remnant of Freud's topographic theory and archeological model for the analytic process (e.g., Freud, 1913). This model fails to take into account the contribution of the analyst's psychological organization in the framing of interpretations. Every transference interpretation—indeed, the very concept of transference itself—is rooted in the theoretical framework that guides the analyst's ordering of the clinical data. Invariably, the analyst's allegiance to his guiding framework has roots in deeply felt personal beliefs and values (Stolorow & Atwood, 1979; Lichtenberg, 1983). Thus each time the analyst offers an interpretation that goes beyond what the patient is consciously aware of, he invites the patient to see things, if ever so slightly, from the analyst's own theory-rooted perspective. To that extent, *interpretations are suggestions,* and it is critical to the analysis to investigate whether the patient believes that he must adopt the analyst's viewpoint in order to maintain the therapeutic bond.

3. The Myth of Uncontaminated Transference

Often the question of whether a psychotherapy can be converted to a psychoanalysis is discussed in terms of whether the psychotherapist's noninterpretive interventions have "contaminated" the transference so as to render it unanalyzable (Panel, 1987). The assumption here is that transference can exist in a form that is "uncontaminated" by the activity of the therapist. This assumption derives from the traditional conceptualization of transference, according to which the patient "displaces emotions belonging to an unconscious representation of a repressed object to a mental representation of an object of the external world" (Nunberg, 1951, p. 1). Lachmann and I (Stolorow & Lachmann, 1984/85) have criticized the concept of transference as displacement as follows:

> The concept of transference as displacement has perpetuated the view that the patient's experience of the analytic relationship is solely a product of the patient's past and psychopathology and has not been determined by the activity (or nonactivity) of the analyst. This viewpoint is consistent with Freud's archeological metaphor. In neglecting the contribution of the analyst to the transference, it contains certain pitfalls. Suppose an archeologist unknowningly dropped a wristwatch into a dig. If the assumption is made that anything found in the dig must have been there beforehand, some woefully unwarranted conclusions would be reached [p. 24].

I agree entirely with Gill's (1984) contention that "the notion that the transference can develop without contamination is an illusion" (p. 175). When transference is conceived not as displacement (or regression, or projection, or distortion), but as an expression of unconscious organizing activity (Stolorow & Lachmann, 1984/85), then it becomes apparent that the transference is shaped *both* by contributions from the analyst *and* the structures of meaning into which these are assimilated by the patient. Transference, in other words, is always evoked by some quality or activity of the analyst that lends itself to being interpreted by the patient according to some developmentally preformed organizing principle.

The contribution of the patient's transference to the production of the analyst's countertransference has found its place within psychoanalytic clinical theory. I am suggesting that the countertransference (broadly conceptualized as a manifestation of the analyst's organizing activity) has a decisive impact in shaping the transference. Transference and countertransference together form an intersubjective system of reciprocal mutual influence (Stolorow et al., 1987). I agree with Gill (1988) that, since the analyst's contribution to the transference is "inevitable and to be analyzed rather than something which can be avoided" (p. 269), conversion from psychotherapy to psychoanalysis in principle poses no special obstacles to the analysis of transference.

I would at this point like to offer my own view of the "intrinsic criteria" (Gill, 1984) that define the essentials of a psychoanalytic process. I propose that psychoanalysis is defined (1) by its central *aim,* (2) by its *investigatory stance,* and (3) by its distinctive *domain of inquiry.*

My collaborators and I (Stolorow et al., 1987) have defined the fundamental aim of a psychoanalytic process as the *unfolding, illumination, and transformation of the patient's subjective world.* We further suggested that the investigatory stance most likely to create a therapeutic situation in which this aim can be maximally achieved is best characterized as an attitude of *sustained empathic inquiry*—one that consistently seeks understanding from within the perspective of the patient's own subjective frame of reference. Such inquiry must include the analyst's continual reflection on the involvement of his own personal subjectivity in the ongoing investigation. Like Gill (1984, 1988), we assume that the distinctive domain of psychoanalytic inquiry, and the one in which its therapeutic action can be found, lies in the investigation of the patient's experience of the analytic relationship—the *analysis of transference.* Such analysis includes the investigation and interpretation of both the selfobject and repetitive/conflictual/resistive dimensions of the transference, as well as the oscillating figure-ground relationships between these two poles of the transference which occur in consequence of shifts in the patient's perception of the analyst and his activities. Since the patient's experience of the analytic relationship is codetermined by the organizing activities of *both* participants in the analytic dialogue, the domain of psychoanalytic investigation must encompass the entire *intersubjective field* created by the interplay between the differently organized subjective worlds of patient and analyst.

Although my description of the intrinsic criteria that define psychoanalysis differs in some respects from Gill's, I agree with his contention that it is the intrinsic criteria, and not "extrinsic" factors such as frequency of sessions or use of the couch, that determine whether or not a therapeutic process is a psychoanalytic one. Furthermore, it cannot be routinely assumed that a prescribed frequency of sessions, recumbency on the couch, or any other feature of standard psychoanalytic procedure will maximally facilitate the unfolding, illumination, and transformation of the patient's subjective world. This can be determined only by careful analytic investigation of the transference meanings these procedures acquire for the patient. Moreover, converting psychotherapy to psychoanalysis does not in principle pose technical problems that substantially differ from those arising from any other contribution of the analyst to the intersubjective system. The transference meanings of the previous nonanalytic procedures, of the newly assumed analytic stance, and of the change from the former to the latter should all be investigated in detail. Finally, employing the intrinsic criteria outlined above, I would fully endorse Gill's (1988) statement that "the question of converting psychotherapy into psychoanalysis should rarely arise in the practice of a psychoanalyst because almost always he should be practicing psychoanalysis" (p. 262).

I turn now to a fourth and final assumption that regularly appears in discussions of converting psychotherapy to psychoanalysis—the assumption that patients can be classified as analyzable or unanalyzable on the basis of assessments of their psychopathology alone (see Tyson & Sandler, 1971).

4. The Myth of the Analyzable (or Unanalyzable) Patient

One of the novel contributions that Kohut (1971) introduced was his approach to diagnosing the presence of narcissistic personality disorder. "The crucial diagnostic criterion," he wrote, "is to be based not on the evaluation of the presenting symptomatology or even of the life history, but on the *nature of the spontaneously developing transference*" (p. 23, emphasis added). If, after a preliminary period in which resistances to the transference were clarified, the patient established an idealizing or mirroring selfobject transference tie to the analyst, then the diagnosis of narcissistic personality disorder could be made. On the basis of the formation of such a transference bond, the patient was also judged to be analyzable, in contrast to borderline and psychotic patients who, at that time, were assumed to be incapable of establishing analyzable transferences.

Subsequent studies (Stolorow et al., 1987) have drawn out the radical implications of this approach to psychodiagnosis. The organization of the transference, as I have emphasized, is not solely a product of the patient's past and intrapsychic mechanisms. The analyst's understanding and interpretive activity have a decisive impact in shaping the transference and codetermining which of its dimensions will occupy the experiential foreground of the analysis. The establishment of an analyzable selfobject transference tie, for example, is a product both of the patient's psychological structures and of the analyst's capacity for specific empathic attunement to the patient's inner world. Diagnoses and assessments of analyzability that are based on transference are, in a very profound sense, relative to the particular patient-analyst dyad—the specific intersubjective system—in which they take form. The context of relatedness established between the patient and analyst plays a *constitutive role* in forming and maintaining the transference configurations that emerge in analysis, just as the arly patterns of intersubjective transaction established between the child and its caregivers play a similar constitutive role in the genesis of psychopathology.

What I am saying about the so-called analyzable (or unanalyzable) patient parallels Winnicott's (1965) remark, "There is no such thing as an infant" (p. 39). Just as infant and maternal care together form an indivisible unit, so analyzability is a property not of the patient alone, but of the patient-analyst system. The question of analyzability cannot be determined solely by an assessment of the patient's psychological organization and psychopathology. What must be assessed is the functioning of the entire intersubjective system, the goodness of fit between what the patient most needs to have understood and what the analyst is capable of understanding. Theoretical advances that enlarge our capacity to gain empathic access to patients' subjective worlds in the same measure broaden the range of patients we consider analyzable. While there are doubtless some patients who could be analyzed only by the most gifted of analysts, I believe that, in principle, anyone with an intact nervous system is analyzable by *someone*.

REFERENCES

Basch, M. (1983). Affect and the analyst. *Psychoanal. Inquiry,* 3:691–703.

Brenner, C. (1976). *Psychoanalytic Technique and Psychic Conflict.* New York: Int. Univ. Press.

Freud, A. (1936). *The Ego and the Mechanisms of Defense. Writings,* 2. New York: Int. Univ. Press, 1966.

Freud, S. (1912). Recommendations to physicians practising psycho-analysis. *S.E.,* 12.

——— (1913). The claims of psycho-analysis to scientific interest. *S.E.,* 13.

——— (1915). Observations on transference-love. *S.E.,* 12.

——— (1919). Lines of advance in psycho-analytic therapy. *S.E.,* 17.

Friedman, L. (1978). Trends in the psychoanalytic theory of treatment. *Psychoanal. Q.,* 47:524–567.

Gill, M. (1984). Psychoanalysis and psychotherapy: A revision. *Int. Rev. Psychoanal.,* 11:161–179.

——— (1988). Converting psychotherapy into psychoanalysis. *Contemp. Psychoanal.,* 24:262–274.

Kohut, H. (1959). Introspection, empathy, and psychoanalysis. *J. Amer. Psychoanal. Assn.,* 7:459–483.

_____ (1971). *The Analysis of the Self.* New York: Int. Univ. Press.

_____ (1977). *The Restoration of the Self.* New York: Int. Univ. Press.

_____ (1980). Reflections on *Advances in Self Psychology.* In: *Advances in Self Psychology,* ed. A. Goldberg. New York: Int. Univ. Press, pp. 473–554.

_____ (1984). *How Does Analysis Cure?* Chicago: Univ. Chicago Press.

Leider, R. (1983). Analytic neutrality—A historical review. *Psychoanal. Inquiry,* 3:665–674.

Lichtenberg, J. (1983). The influence of values and value judgments on the psychoanalytic encounter. *Psychoanal. Inquiry,* 3:647–664.

Nunberg, H. (1951). Transference and reality. *Internat. J. Psychoanal.,* 32:1–9.

Panel (1987). Conversion of Psychotherapy to Psychoanalysis, C. P. Fisher, Reporter. *J. Amer. Psychoanal. Assn.,* 35:713–726.

Stolorow, R. & Atwood, G. (1979). *Faces in a Cloud: Subjectivity in Personality Theory.* New York: Jason Aronson.

_____ Brandchaft, B., & Atwood, G. (1987). *Psychoanalytic Treatment: An Intersubjective Approach.* Hillsdale, N.J.: The Analytic Press.

_____ & Lachmann, F. (1984/85). Transference: The future of an illusion. *Ann. Psychoanal.,* 12/13:19–37.

Stone, L. (1961). *The Psychoanalytic Situation.* New York: Int. Univ. Press.

Tyson, R. & Sandler, J. (1971). Problems in the selection of patients for psychoanalysis. *Brit. J. Med. Psychol.,* 44:211–228.

Winnicott, D. (1965). *The Maturational Processes and the Facilitating Environment.* New York: Int. Univ. Press.

Wolf, E. (1976). Ambience and abstinence. *Ann. Psychoanal.,* 4:101–115.

_____ (1983). Aspects of neutrality. *Psychoanal. Inquiry,* 3:675–689.

11726 San Vicente Blvd.
Suite 410
Los Angeles, CA 90049

Conversion of Psychotherapy to Psychoanalysis: The Policies of the Institutes of the American

G. W. PIGMAN III, Ph.D.

ANALYSTS TRAINED AS RECENTLY AS A decade ago recall being discouraged or even prohibited from converting patients they had been seeing in psychotherapy into psychoanalytic control cases. Today one often hears that a decline in the numbers of patients presenting themselves for analysis has led to a change in the practices of many analysts, who now start patients in once- or twice-a-week therapy and then convert them to analysis. Moreover, the American Psychoanalytic Association has made its acceptance of conversion more explicit, although this position does not appear to be as well known as it should be. To learn more about their current policies I made a survey of the institutes of the American concerning conversion. The results may be useful, since at least one institute does not realize that the American looks more favorably on conversion now than in the past.

I asked the chairmen of the education committees whether their institutes allow control cases to be converted, what conditions govern conversion, and whether their policies have changed over the past 10 to 20 years. All of the institutes that responded to my inquiries—24 of the 26—allow conversion. No institute has a formal policy, and most treat conversion as one of the many

Dr. Pigman is Associate Professor of Literature, California Institute of Technology, and a graduate of the Southern California Psychoanalytic Institute.

possible issues to be discussed with a supervisor or to be presented to a case selection committee before deciding to take a patient into analysis. Although all the institutes allow conversion, a wide range of attitudes exists. Some institutes barely tolerate conversion; others encourage it.

St. Louis discourages conversion; Cleveland urges candidates to take patients who have had no previous therapy, especially with themselves; San Diego allows conversion, but says it does not frequently occur; Cincinnati and Michigan prefer that the first two cases have no previous contact with the analyst; Boston prefers one case without previous contact; Denver prefers one or two cases without previous contact, but encourages candidates to convert another, and likes candidates to have the benefit of supervision of the process; Washington prefers that only one case be converted; New York estimates that a candidate would convert no more than one control case and considers conversion in a course on analyzability; San Francisco and Houston by no means object to conversion, but might be concerned if all a candidate's cases were converted; NYU encourages candidates to look through their practices for cases to convert and discusses conversion in seminars on selection and analyzability; Southern California encourages conversion.

New Orleans does the most to encourage conversion and is the only institute to say that it has always encouraged conversion. (The other institutes that responded to the question concerning change in policy say that they are now more open to conversion.) New Orleans prefers not to run a clinic because it believes that candidates select just as good, if not better, patients for analysis from their practices as they would get through a clinic. Candidates are encouraged to assess each patient in their practice as a possible analytic case, and the institute regards it as a cause for concern if a candidate cannot find a suitable patient. The institute advises, although it does not require, candidates to seek analytic supervision for their therapy patients, partially with an eye to converting some of them to analysis. Candidates are urged to examine the kinds of interactions that have taken place with their therapy patients to see whether nonanalytic techniques such as giving advice may have precluded the development of an analytic process, and candidates are advised to refer patients to their colleagues if their previous actions in therapy become too great a source of resistance in the analysis. On balance, analysts in New Orleans would rather take a chance with a patient because they have seen too many exceptions to feel comfortable with hard and fast rules. New Orleans is proud of its 35-year-old attitude toward conversion and feels that this attitude has helped its graduates maintain a high percentage of analytic cases within their practices.

All of the institutes agree that the length of time the patient is in psychotherapy is a factor in making a decision to convert, but none regards it as an overriding factor, and none specifies a time limit. (Los Angeles reports that some patients have had two to three years of therapy with the analyst before conversion to analysis.) Assessing the possibility of developing an analyzable transference neurosis is the most pressing concern for most institutes, and previous therapy is scrutinized for departures from a neutral stance (supportive measures, direct advice) or other parameters that might impede the development of a transference neurosis.

A few institutes say that they have liberalized their stance in response to changes within the American, and some express the opinion that these changes are due to the decreasing number of patients presenting themselves for analysis. Whatever the reasons, the American has tried to publicize its acceptance of conversion under certain conditions. At a workshop on certification at the meeting of the American, December 17, 1987, the chairman and a member of the Committee on Certification were asked, "What about patients with prior therapy?" (memorandum to candidates, affiliate, associate, and extended associate members of the American, June 14, 1988). They replied, "We do see that more. The committee does not have a prejudice against cases with prior therapy with the same therapist. We are interested in your thinking about the transition from one form of therapy to the other, what led to the decision, the effect of therapy on the analysis. It might be that you would not want to treat the patient you had had in therapy if interventions had to be made that would put the analyst in a difficult situation and might hinder the unfolding of the transference, etc. It would depend on the interaction. In some cases it would be better to refer the patient to a colleague. Or you might feel the earlier therapy was preparation for the analysis. Again, it's not a clear cut rule." And in response to my inquiry, Shelley Orgel, the chairman of the Board of Professional Standards of the American, reaffirmed the American's acceptance of conversion and stated the issues surrounding conversion succinctly: "The essential requirement is that the candidate demonstrate an understanding and appreciation of the factors which may be a part of psychotherapy—the nature of the therapeutic relationship, the kinds of interventions made, the 'intrusion' of the real person of the therapist on future transference development, the amount and kinds of gratifications which would then have to be curtailed in the interest of the analysis—which would have a negative impact on the likelihood that that therapist could successfully bring the analysis of *that* patient to an *analytic* conclusion."

When asked to survey the institutes, I did not have strong feelings about conversion one way or another, but in the course of conducting the survey I came to feel that conversion should become more explicitly an educational issue rather than something to tolerate in less favorable circumstances. I hope that the results of this survey may encourage some institutes to reconsider their *educational* stance towards conversion. Since conversion is a fact of the current analytic scene, it seems to me that the institutes that encourage candidates to look for patients to convert, supervise them through the process, and bring it up in case seminars and courses on analyzability or case selection deserve to be commended for helping their candidates face the realities of contemporary analytic practice.

California Institute of Technology 104-40
Pasadena, CA 91125

Epilogue

THE PRECEDING PAPERS COVER a wide range of concerns in the conversion of psychotherapy to psychoanalysis. A method of study of the problem was described. Resistances to psychoanalysis on the part of both the patient and the analyst were examined. There was a discussion of patients originally considered unsuitable for psychoanalysis, who became suitable with psychotherapy, and a case example was given. The idea that the original psychotherapy can be similar to the beginning of any analytic process was considered. Some of the assumptions regarding the nature of the psychoanalytic process which have a bearing on conversion were questioned.

The contributors accept the proposition that the conversion of psychotherapy to psychoanalysis is a legitimate endeavor, even with the same therapist, and is not necessarily doomed to failure. The survey of the institutes of the American Psychoanalytic Association indicated that conversion is now relatively routine for required supervisory cases for candidates.

Conversion of psychotherapy to psychoanalysis has clearly become a common procedure. The contributions to this issue of *Psychoanalytic Inquiry* have sought to expand our understanding of the process. The change might well be based on economic considerations and the availability of cases, or perhaps on the widening scope; in any event, the overall direction seems to be toward approving conversion to analysis with the same therapist.

Arthur Malin, M.D.
Issue Editor

TOPICS OF FUTURE ISSUES

Corrective Emotional Experience Revisited

How Theory Shapes Technique: Self Psychology

The Child and the Adult: Similarities, Dissimilarities, and Continuities

Separation-Inviduation Theory Revisited

Psychoanalysis and Neuroscience

Female Issues

How the Analyst's Work Shapes the Analyst

The Significance of Gender for Transference and Countertransference

Ten Years of Inquiry by Psychoanalysts: The Decade of the Eighties

Ethics in the World Community

Interpretation and Its Consequences

Phobia

Erotic Transferences

For Product Safety Concerns and Information please contact our EU
representative GPSR@taylorandfrancis.com
Taylor & Francis Verlag GmbH, Kaufingerstraße 24, 80331 München, Germany

www.ingramcontent.com/pod-product-compliance
Lightning Source LLC
LaVergne TN
LVHW010621300926
849162LV00001B/27
* 9 7 8 0 8 8 1 6 3 9 5 5 1 *